Pearson Education
Test Prep Series
for
AP® HUMAN GEOGRAPHY

To accompany:

The Cultural Landscape

AN INTRODUCTION
TO HUMAN GEOGRAPHY

AP® EDITION, 11TH EDITION

James M. Rubenstein

Prepared by

Shanna L. Hurt

John Philip Antony Hurt

PEARSON

Boston   Columbus   Indianapolis   New York   San Francisco   Upper Saddle River
Amsterdam   Cape Town   Dubai   London   Madrid   Milan   Munich   Paris   Montréal   Toronto
Delhi   Mexico City   São Paulo   Sydney   Hong Kong   Seoul   Singapore   Taipei   Tokyo

Senior Geography Editor: Christian Botting

Senior Marketing Manager: Maureen McLaughlin

Assistant Editor: Kristen Sanchez

Senior Marketing Assistant: Nicola Houston

Managing Editor, Geosciences and Chemistry: Gina M. Cheselka

Project Manager: Janice Stangel

Supplement Cover Designer: Seventeenth Street Studios

Operations Specialist: Christy Hall

Cover Photo Credit: Picture Contact BV/Alamy

AP® is a trademark registered and/or owned by the College Board, which was not involved in the production of, and does not endorse, this product.

Please visit our Web site at
www.PearsonSchool.com/Advanced

ISBN-13: 978-0-13-309596-8
ISBN-10: 0-13-309596-7

Table of Contents

Introduction to AP Human Geography

Advanced Placement Human Geography is an introductory college course in human geography. The exam assumes that you have taken the equivalent of one semester of college-level preparation, with the understanding that many high schools will teach the course for one year, depending on their schedules.

Geographers who are members of the AP Human Geography Development Committee have selected all material on the exam. The material included in this guide correlates to what they feel is a typical introductory college course in human geography. The exam at the end of the school year is representative of this material and is considered an appropriate measure of skills and knowledge needed in the field of introductory human geography.

The prescribed curriculum for this course is outlined by The College Board, and it gives you a learning experience similar to what you would obtain in a college level introductory human geography course. It is at the discretion of the school to develop the course to work into its existing schedule.

The purpose of this course is to introduce you to the systematic study of patterns and processes that have shaped human understanding, use, and alteration of Earth's surface. As a geography student, you will look spatially at the Earth to analyze humans' organization of space and the environmental consequences of their decisions. You will be looking for patterns across the cultural landscape, trying to identify trends and then anticipate future phenomena that might occur across the landscape. You will also explore different methods and tools geographers use in their science and practice.

Goals of AP Human Geography

AP Human Geography was established with five college-level goals in mind. These goals are aligned directly with the National Geography Standards that were developed in 1994. Upon successful completion of the course, you should have developed geographic skills that enable you to:

Use and think about maps and spatial data.

Maps and spatial data are essential in discovering patterns on Earth's surface that reflect and influence physical and human processes. Learning to use and think critically with these tools will allow you to use real world data to problem solve various situations on Earth. Thinking critically about what is obvious and also that which is hidden on various maps, gives you the understanding you need to successfully use maps and spatial data.

Understand and interpret the implications of associations among phenomena in places.

Geographers look at data and map sets in order to understand changes in the spatial organization of Earth's surface. They are particularly interested in focusing on how phenomena (*an observable fact, occurrence, or circumstance*) are related to one another in particular places. You should be able to not only recognize and interpret patterns, but also to identify the nature and significance of the relationships among phenomena that occur in the same place. In addition, you should understand how a culture's values and tastes, political situations, and economic conditions help to create unique cultural landscapes.

Recognize and interpret at different scales the relationships among patterns and processes.

Geographic study also requires that you view patterns at different scales. Geography really is a matter of scale. You should understand that a phenomenon looked at on a local scale could very well be influenced by circumstances occurring at another scale—national, local, or even global. You should look for the connections operating at multiple scales when trying to explain geographic patterns and arrangements.

Define regions and evaluate the regionalization process.

Geography is not only concerned with identifying patterns across the cultural landscape, but also with analyzing how they came about and what they mean. To successfully make such an analysis, you need to break the patterns into smaller parts or categories, referred to as regions. By looking critically at regions of the world, you will be able to consider how and why the regions emerged and hypothesize the implications for future development of Earth's surface.

Characterize and analyze changing interconnections among places.

To obtain the true depth of the geographic perspective, you must understand that events and processes occurring in one place can have a profound influence on other places. You should look at places and patterns as part of a whole, not in isolation. Be aware that relationships on Earth are in constant motion, they are continually changing, and your job is to figure out how and why this change occurs.

Topics in AP Human Geography

I. Geography: Its Nature and Perspectives

This course emphasizes geography as a field of academic study and gives a brief overview of geography in nineteenth-century Europe. This overview will show how the discipline has evolved into the study of diverse cultures and unique areas organized around some key concepts.

You will be introduced to the importance of spatial organization—the location of places, people, and events on Earth. In addition you will look for the global connections of places and landscapes in order to understand human activity across Earth's surface.

Key concepts that will be important throughout the course are location, space, place, scale, pattern, regionalization, and globalization. These concepts are essential for your understanding of spatial interaction and spatial organization of Earth's surface. You should be able to successfully analyze human population growth and movement, cultural patterns, economic use of the Earth, political organization of space, and human settlement patterns, especially urbanization. You will learn how to use and interpret maps to make these analyses. The course will allow you to apply mathematical formulas, models, and qualitative date to these geographic concepts in order to make educated predictions. The course will also ask that you make regional analysis of various phenomena and create appropriate regions to illustrate certain processes.

Ultimately, this course should allow you to see the relevance of academic geography in everyday life and decision-making. You should be able to apply these key concepts when looking at current events and policies. You should be able to ask yourself the following questions: "If I were a policy maker for the United Nations, why would this information be important? How would I use it to develop public policy that would impact humans in sub-Saharan Africa, Europe, and North America?"

II: Population

An important geographic concept is how populations are organized over Earth's surface. This part of the course gives you the tools you need to make sense of cultural, political, economic, and urban systems. By analyzing demographic data such as infant mortality rates, crude death rates, crude birth rates, and migration, you will understand the distribution of human population at different scales: global, continental, national, state and local community. You will be able to explain why populations are growing or declining in certain places and not others. You will be asked to discover where and why fertility rates have dropped in some parts of the developing world, but not in others. Look at how age-sex structures (population pyramids) are different in many regions of the world and explain the political, cultural, economic implications of these differences. A key component of population geography that is important in today's world is your understanding of refugee flows, immigration (both internal and out-migration) and residential mobility (movement to the Sunbelt) in order to appreciate the interconnectedness of our world. The relationship between refugees and political boundaries is also important, especially where refugees have no access to political power because they find themselves "on the wrong side of the line." Another key concept related to populations is that of environmental degradation. With increases in regional populations, many stresses occur on the environment, thus causing rapid out-migration and urbanization. Rapid immigration to certain parts of the world can exacerbate antiforeigner sentiment because of the imbalance that occurs in wages, employment, and political power. You will also compare different models of population change, including demographic and epidemiological transitions, and government population policies. Upon completion of this unit, you should be able to evaluate the role, strengths and weaknesses of major population policies and make recommendations regarding them. For instance, is education essential in lowering fertility rates? Should females be empowered to accomplish this?

III. Cultural Patterns and Processes

Critical to your understanding of human geography is your ability to analyze and predict various components of regional cultural patterns and processes. To be successful in doing this you will be learning about the concept of culture. What is culture? What makes up a person's culture? We begin by looking at the spatial distribution of cultural groups as defined by their language, religion, race, ethnicity, and gender. It is vital to look at the past and the present in your analysis, as the spatial distribution of these characteristics changes over time.

You must look at cultural patterns from a variety of geographic scales, starting with local and then moving to the global scale. Diffusion is a key concept when you are looking at these patterns. For example, you might look at the location of certain agricultural processes, or housing types, or where certain religions or languages are practiced. How did these traits get from point A to point B? Your job is to analyze these patterns of diffusion.

In this analysis the concept of folk culture versus popular culture will emerge. This is an important way to differentiate between cultures. Folk cultures tend to be isolated and will only diffuse through relocation, like the Amish culture. Popular cultures are global and relocate through many different types of diffusion. You will be able to distinguish between the languages and dialects, religious practices, ethnic and universalizing religions, as well as the popular or folk culture of a group. This will lead to your understanding of geographic patterns. You will see that each culture leaves a unique imprint on the landscape.

One important aspect of this section of the course is to look at the way culture shapes human-environmental relationships. The root word for culture is *cultus (to care for),* so when making your analysis of what a cultural group cares about, look around. If someone visits a major city in the United States, what would they see—NFL football stadiums, NBA stadiums, NBL fields? This cultural landscape reflects what people in that culture do with their spare time and money. Would the landscape look the same in different regions, like the Middle East or Europe? Landscapes tend to reflect the cultural values, tastes and sets of beliefs of a group of people. By looking at these landscapes you should be able to identify cultural traits, such as the language and religion of a group of people. This will help you to build a cultural map of the group. Where did they begin, where did they move to, where are they now, where will they be in the future?

IV. Political Organization of Space

This section of the course will introduce you to the political organization of Earth's surface at a variety of scales. You need to keep in mind that the political boundaries that have been drawn over the years reflect somebody's view of how Earth should be divided. This view is sometimes in conflict with other's views of where a boundary should be and thus problems can occur.

The main emphasis is on the concept of a "nation-state" or country. How did the current world map emerge? What political entities were at play to get the boundaries we have today? You will be looking at the world in historic terms, so that you might be able to analyze these changes over time. For example, you should be able to see the impact of colonialism on these boundaries, as well as the devolution of the former Soviet Union. You will notice that often there is no correlation between ethnic, economic, or environmental patterns and the contemporary world map. You will consider forces that are changing the role of individual nation-states in the contemporary world, like ethnic conflicts, supranationalism, economic globalization, regional economic blocs, and the need to confront environmental issues that know no political boundaries.

To truly understand the complexities associated with political boundaries, you must look at the issues at different scales, such as political units above and below the state. Political units above the state level would be regional alliances, such as NATO, the European Union, or the United Nations. If you wanted to look at the scale below the state, then you would be analyzing entities like city boundaries, ethnic boundaries, and voting districts. In addition, you will study how specific policies affect the spatial organization of cultural and social life, such as racial segregation.

V. Agricultural and Rural Land Use

In this portion of the course you will explore four basic themes: the origin and diffusion of agriculture, key characteristics of the world's agricultural regions, reasons why these regions function the way they do, and the environmental impact of agriculture. First, it is important to examine where domesticated agricultural practices began and look at the diffusion of these practices around the globe. You will understand the impacts of diet, energy use, and new technologies on the emergence of sedentary societies.

Next, you will look at Earth's major agricultural production regions. You will examine both extensive activity (fishing, forestry, nomadic herding, ranching, and shifting cultivation), and intensive activity (plantation agriculture, mixed crop/livestock systems, market gardening, factory farms, and horticulture). You will also be concerned with land survey systems, environmental conditions, and cultural values that create and sustain these patterns.

One theory that will be important to your understanding of explanations for the location of agricultural activities is Von Thunen's agricultural land use model. Other agricultural activities such as the impact of factory farming on food supplies, and the distribution of crops and animals are also emphasized. The need to increase food production concludes your study of agriculture. What will be the impact of genetically modified crops (biotechnology) on food production?

VI. Industrialization and Economic Development

Economic activity can be analyzed by looking at the interaction of natural resources, culture, politics, and history in specific places. It is this interaction that allows you to get a spatial perspective of areas across our cultural landscape. By looking at these key concepts (natural resources, culture, politics, history), you will be able to appreciate why resources have different values in different societies around the globe. These values give regions comparative advantages for development over other regions.

Economic development models will be studied throughout this unit. You will look at Rostow's stages of economic growth, where he argued that countries will go through five stages of development, beginning with traditional societies and ending with a nation characterized by high mass consumption. By looking at Immanuel Wallerstein's World Systems Theory (core-periphery), you will be able to explain why the world has emerged into a well-developed core and a less-developed periphery. During this time you will compare location theories, such as Weber and von Thunen, in order to understand if these theories are still valid in our ever-globalizing world. Does time-space compression still hold true? Why have Asian markets flourished, while sub-Saharan markets have declined? What is the impact of economic growth on North America? Why is that region in decline?

You will also be looking at contemporary issues that surround economic activity. By looking at these issues at various scales, you will see how new patterns of economic inequity emerge. How will certain communities or countries deal with pollution and the quality of life? What will be the impact of deindustrialization, the disaggregation of production, and the rise of consumption and leisure activities on the community, the country, and the region?

VII. Cities and Urban Land Use

The urban geography unit focuses on the development and character of cities, and the internal structure and landscape of urban areas. To appreciate the study of cities, you will look at historical and current locations of cities, as well as their political, economic, and cultural functions. You will also analyze transportation and communications among cities, and begin to understand why there are differences in the growth of cities. Many of these differences will be tied to their political, economic, or cultural traits. Theories that will be examined during this first part of the unit will be Christaller's central place theory, the rank size rule, and the gravity model. Quantitative information, such as demographic data, migration, zones of influence, or the effects of job creation programs are used to analyze changes in the urban hierarchy.

The second focus will be on the internal structure and landscapes of urban areas. You will be evaluating what it would be like to live and work in a large city. You will be looking at land use patterns, racial and ethnic segregation, and transportation systems within the city, architecture patterns, and cycles of development. Within this study, you will continue to use qualitative data from the census bureau, as well as qualitative information that you will collect from narrative accounts and field studies. You will be presented with different models of internal city structure: the Burgess concentric zone model, the Hoyt sector model, and the Harris-Ullman multiple nuclei model. *{Note: sometimes on the AP Exam, these models might only be called by the model name, like sector model, instead of Hoyt sector model.)* When studying these models it is important for you to look at the architectural history and emergence of transportation within the city to truly appreciate the city's cultural landscape.

You will study new trends in urban development, such as the emergence of edge cities and the gentrification of neighborhoods. You will be looking at new types of urban planning initiatives and community actions that help shape the future of cities.

Although most urban geographers focus on North American cities, it will be important for you to compare urban structures in other parts of the world. The study of European, Islamic, East and South Asian, Latin American, and sub-Saharan African cities can illustrate the cultural values and economic systems of different regions. This will help you to see the spatial distribution and patterns that have been prevalent throughout this course.

The AP Exam

The AP Human Geography exam is about 2 hours and 15 minutes in length and includes both a 60-minute multiple-choice section and a 75-minute free-response section. Each section accounts for half of the student's exam grade.

The following are the approximate percentages of the multiple-choice section that are devoted to each area:

I. Geography: Its Nature and Perspectives	5–10%
II. Population	13–17%
III. Cultural Patterns and Processes	13–17%
IV. Political Organization of Space	13–17%
V. Agriculture and Rural Land Use	13–17%
VI. Industrialization and Economic Development	13–17%
VII. Cities and Urban Land Use	13–17%

Your exam score is converted into The College Board AP Central's 5-point scale as follows:

5   Extremely well qualified

4   Well qualified

3   Qualified

2   Possibly qualified

1   No recommendation

Strategies for Success in AP Human Geography

1. Thinking geographically

Much of the content of this course deals with themes and issues that are integral to our world today. For example, population policies, political conflicts between and within countries, and the problems of suburban sprawl are all regular newsworthy items. The key is to think about current events in geographical terms. Students should always consider the spatial aspects of world events. For example, in a conflict between two countries, the geographical importance lies in understanding boundary disputes, the location of different ethnic groups, conflict over land and resources, and infrastructural considerations. This way of thinking should be imprinted throughout the course.

2. Using and interpreting graphs, maps, and charts

The textbook contains numerous graphics, especially maps. It is critical that students practice reading and interpreting these maps. Make sure that they understand the title, key, and scale, and can describe what the map is showing. Specific graphics must be understood. For example, what does a population pyramid show? There will be graphs, maps, and charts on the Advanced Placement Human Geography examination, both in the multiple-choice section and the free-response questions. This guide includes activities and free-response questions that integrate graphs, maps, and charts so that students can practice reading and interpreting them.

3. Integrating the content

In the high school social studies curriculum, we tend to think in compartments such as history, geography, economics, and politics. Within this course, we do the same thing, and consider topics such as political geography, industry and development, and urbanization. It is imperative that students have a more holistic way of thinking before they go into the examination. For example, ethnicity and political geography overlap. Population is relevant to urbanization, and development incorporates material from other units in the course. Some of the free-response questions on the examination will require students to draw information from a number of different units, and so they must integrate the content.

4. Knowledge and use of case studies

In both sections of the examination, students will be required to answer questions that involve a specific knowledge and understanding of different places in the world. On the free-response section they may have to exemplify a concept with a specific example. Thus a working knowledge of case studies is essential. These may include the Middle East, the Balkans and the breakup of Yugoslavia, ethnic and political conflict in the Caucasus, or the political boundaries of Africa. In each of the above case studies, there are geographic issues that transcend specific chapters in the text. For example, students should be familiar with population, religious, ethnic, political, and economic aspects of regional case studies as appropriate.

5. A broad geographical knowledge

More than any other geography course, Advanced Placement Human Geography requires students to think and write critically in the content area. This should not take away from the fact that they also need to have a working knowledge of world political geography. For example, they should be expected to have a pretty good idea of which countries colonized different parts of the developing world, and the characteristics of different regions of the globe. Can students identify the major countries in each region or realm of the world? In the context of higher-level questions, the examination will still require this knowledge. For example, a map that accompanies a free-response question will often show political boundaries without showing the names of countries, and students will be expected to identify these countries correctly.

6. Knowledge and use of models

Models are integral to human geography, and students need to be familiar with them. These include but are not limited to the demographic and migration transition, models of industrial location and agricultural land use, development models, central place theory, and models of urban structure. Students should know the title, content, and author of the model together with the underlying assumptions. Where they deviate from reality, students need to be able to explain those differences. To what extent is the model useful in explaining spatial reality in that context? Students' knowledge of models in human geography will be tested on the examination. It is always possible that one of the free-response questions will focus on a specific model.

7. Material from a variety of texts and other support materials

This textbook covers most of the key concepts and content areas of the course. The correlation guide aligns every part of the Advanced Placement Human Geography outline to key issues throughout the text. The key vocabulary terms are highlighted and defined in the textbook, and highlighted again in this guide. Together they provide the necessary content for success in the course. At the same time it must be realized that the examiners are not working from this text alone. Thus it is the instructor's responsibility to make sure that students are exposed to some other materials and texts as part of the preparation for the examination. This guide has made every effort to contain a review of all the content and vocabulary that might be part of the Advanced Placement Human Geography examination, including material that is only briefly mentioned or not covered in Rubenstein's text.

8. Review and exam preparation

This guide is a comprehensive review and examination preparation manual. Students need to take the practice tests under exam conditions. The guide includes two multiple-choice examinations of 75 questions each, together with six free-response questions. On the multiple-choice section they need to read the entire question and use a process of elimination. There is no penalty for guessing, so students should answer all questions on the multiple-choice portion.

On the free-response questions students should read the question, underlining key terms, and then spend a few minutes jotting down ideas and making an outline that will help them to answer it. If a question is organized A, B, and C, make sure their answer follows the same format. Introductory and concluding paragraphs are not necessary; students should get to the point quickly and be as succinct as possible. Recognize what the question is asking. One that asks a student to evaluate or analyze involves more, and will be worth more points than one where the task is to list or describe. Use specific examples where asked to do so. There are three free-response questions on the exam, each of which must be answered (unlike some Advanced Placement examinations there is no choice). Some questions will deal with content material specific to one unit while others will require students to draw upon material from more than one unit. It is always in the student's best interest to make connection from many different units, when possible, as geographic units and concepts are not "stand alone", but rather are interwoven.

On both sections of the examination they should be cognizant of the time limit throughout. On the multiple-choice part of the exam, students should come back to questions where they are unsure. On the free-response questions, students should answer the question(s) about which they are most confident first, leaving what they consider to be the most difficult to last. It is imperative that they try to answer all the questions.

About the Authors

John P.A. Hurt graduated from Durham University, UK, with a BA (Honours) degree in Geography in 1982. He completed his MEd in Secondary Education and MA in History at the University of Missouri in St. Louis. John is a Fellow and Chartered Geographer with the United Kingdom's Royal Geographical Society and Institute of British Geographers. He received the National Council for Geographic Education's Distinguished Teaching Award in 1999. After many years in Littleton Public Schools (Colorado) John has been teaching geography and history at Seoul International School since 2010, and Advanced Placement Human Geography since 2000. John is an Endorsed Consultant with The College Board and conducts workshops for AP Human Geography teachers in their Western Region.

Shanna L. Hurt graduated from the University of Texas with a BS degree in Political Science and Secondary Education in 1987. She completed her Master's degree in Geography at East Texas State University. Shanna received the National Council for Geographic Education's Distinguished Teaching Award in 2001. After teaching many years in the United States, Shanna has been teaching geography, history, and economics at Seoul International School since 2010, and Advanced Placement Human Geography since 2002. Shanna has been a reader for the AP Human Geography exam since 2006, and has written test items for this exam.

To the Student

Preparing for the AP Human Geography Exam

I. Stay organized and keep up with current events. You should get a notebook and take notes, not only on your teacher's lectures, but also on reading assignments you are given. The use of study groups in a great way to make sure you understand the content. In our digital age, some students find it helpful to create a Google doc to share with their friends, so that you can ask questions of each other and comment on questions that may arise. Every single unit you study is illustrated daily on the news. Get in the habit of looking at the world news and making connections with what you are learning in class.

II. Use AP Central's web site: http://www.apcentral.collegeboard.com
This site gives you valuable information about the exam, as well as sample multiple choice and free response questions. The more you are exposed to different types of questions, the better. You will also use this website to register to receive your scores after the exam.

III. APHG multiple-choice questions:
There will be 75 multiple-choice questions, each with 5 choices on your exam. You will have 60 minutes to answer all 75. You should **answer those you know first**, then go back to the ones you are unsure of. **There is no penalty for guessing,** so you should try to answer all of the questions. This portion of the test consists of 50% of your score.

IV. APHG free response questions:
There will be **three** free response questions on your exam. Most of the time two out of the three will include some sort of graphic, maybe a map, photo, population pyramid or chart. The questions that are formatted, A., B., C., where they ask you to explain or do something, should be answered in that format.

For example if there is a question:
A. Define urbanization.

Your answer should be:
A. Urbanization is the process by which the population of cities grows, both in *numbers* and *percentage*.

Make sure that you **underline** all required parts of the prompt. Important words that are commonly used might ask that you **define** and **explain**, or **interpret** from information given. A common problem that occurs is that you might do one, such as define, and not the other, such as explain. You will be given a point for the definition, but will not receive a point for the explanation, so it is important to answer all that is being asked of you. As with the multiple choice section, **answer the free response question that you know for sure, FIRST,** then go on to the other ones. **There is no penalty for attempting to answer a free response question.** Try to bring in concepts from all units of APHG whenever possible. The free response portion of the test is 50% of your score. Use your best penmanship, so that you don't lose points because the reader cannot read your writing.

Example of a free response question with appropriate answer:

South Korea is experiencing a large elderly population.
A. Describe and explain two potential problems that arise in countries with aging populations.
B. Identify and explain potential government strategies that might address this problem.

Potential Answer:
A. Countries that are experiencing aging or graying populations such as South Korea, Japan, or Italy are faced with many problems. One potential problem deals with the dependency ratio (or the number of people too young or too old to work). In countries with a large number of old people, they are not working and contributing to the economy of the country, and this puts a strain on things such as Social Security because not enough people are paying in, but many are taking out. Second, these countries have a very low birth rate and will soon face not having enough skilled workers to contribute in the economy. The country might have to become dependent on immigrant workers, who are culturally different from them.

B. Governments need to address this problem by encouraging people to have children. They might give incentives for couples that have children, such as tax breaks or even pay them to have children. They could also increase the retirement age, making people work longer so that there is less strain on social benefits.

A poor attempt to the questions might look like this:
A. Two problems that this country will face is:
1. too many old people not enough young people
2. an unbalance population pyramid

B. The government should allow more illegal immigrants to come in.

V. Registering for the exam:
If your school offers AP, contact your AP Coordinator to register for the exams. He or she will order the necessary materials, collect fees, and let you know when and where to appear for the exams.

The AP Human Geography exam fee is currently $89.

If for some reason you want to cancel your AP Human Geography score and have it permanently removed from your records, you should fill out a score cancellation form and send it to College Board.

Correlation Guide for the National Geography Standards and *The Cultural Landscape: An Introduction to Human Geography*, AP Edition 11e textbook

Listed below are the eighteen National Geography Standards as they correlate to the key issues in each chapter of the textbook:

<u>National Geography Standards</u>	<u>Textbook Chapters and Key Issues</u>
1. How to use maps and other geographic representations, geospatial technologies, and spatial thinking to understand and communicate information	Chapter 1 Key Issues 1, 2, and 3
2. How to use mental maps to organize information about people, places, and environments in a spatial context	Chapter 1 Key Issue 2
3. How to analyze the spatial organization of people, places, and environments on Earth's surface	Chapter 1 Key Issues 1 and 3 Chapter 7 Key Issues 1 and 2 Chapter 8 Key Issues 1 and 2 Chapter 9 Key Issues 1 and 2
4. The physical and human characteristics of place	Chapter 1 Key Issue 3 Chapter 11 Key Issue 2
5. That people create regions to interpret Earth's complexity	Chapter 1 Key Issue 2
6. How culture and experience influence people's perceptions of places and regions	Chapter 1 Key Issue 2
7. The physical processes that shape the patterns of Earth's surface	Chapter 1 Key Issue 4
8. The characteristics and spatial distribution of ecosystems and biomes on Earth's surface	Chapter 1 Key Issue 4 Chapter 10 Key issue 3
9. The characteristics, distribution, and migration of human populations on Earth's surface	Chapter 2 Key Issues 1, 2, and 3 Chapter 3 Key Issues 1, 2, 3, and 4
10. The characteristics, distribution, and complexity of Earth's cultural mosaics	Chapter 4 Key Issues 1, 2, 3, and 4 Chapter 5 Key Issues 1, 2, 3, and 4 Chapter 6 Key Issues 1, 2, and 3
11. The patterns and networks of economic interdependence on Earth's surface	Chapter 9 Key Issue 4 Chapter 10 Key Issue 4 Chapter 11 Key Issues 2 and 4 Chapter 12 Key Issues 2 and 3

12. The processes, patterns, and functions of human settlement	Chapter 12 Key Issues 1, 2, 3, and 4 Chapter 13 Key Issues 1, 2, 3 and 4
13. How the forces of cooperation and conflict among people influence the division and control of Earth's surface	Chapter 6 Key Issue 4 Chapter 7 Key Issues 3 and 4 Chapter 8 Key Issues 3 and 4
14. How human actions modify the physical environment	Chapter 1 Key Issue 4 Chapter 10 Key Issues 1, 2, 3 and 4 Chapter 11 Key Issue 3
15. How physical systems affect human systems	Chapter 10 Key Issues 1, 2, 3 and 4
16. The changes that occur in the meaning, use, distribution, and importance of resources	Chapter 1 Key Issue 4 Chapter 9 Key Issue 3 Chapter 11 Key Issue 2
17. How to apply geography to interpret the past	Chapter 5 Key Issue 2 Chapter 6 Key Issue 2 Chapter 8 Key Issue 4 Chapter 10 Key Issue 1 Chapter 11 Key Issue 1 Chapter 12 Key Issue 4
18. How to apply geography to interpret the present and plan for the future	Chapter 1 Key Issue 4 Chapter 2 Key Issue 4 Chapter 3 Key Issue 4 Chapter 4 Key Issue 4 Chapter 8 Key Issue 4 Chapter 9 Key Issue 4 Chapter 10 Key Issue 4 Chapter 11 Key Issue 4 Chapter 13 Key Issue 4

Chapter

1 Basic Concepts

How Do Geographers Describe Where Things Are?

Learning Outcome 1.1.1: Explain differences between early maps and contemporary maps.

Some of the earliest maps were used for navigation. Maps have had many other uses as tools of reference and communication.

Learning Outcome 1.1.2: Describe the role of map scale and projections in making maps.

Contemporary maps indicate scale in three ways. Four types of distortion can occur in the transfer of Earth's round surface to a flat map.

Learning Outcome 1.1.3: Explain how latitude and longitude are used to locate points on Earth's surface.

Latitude indicates position north or south of the equator, and longitude indicates position east or west of the prime meridian.

Learning Outcome 1.1.4: Identify contemporary analytic tools, including remote sensing, GPS, and GIS.

Geographers today use the tools of Geographic Information Science (GIScience). Data gathered by remote sensing and GPS to measure changes over time and the characteristics of places can be combined and analyzed using geographic information systems (GIS).

Human geographers ask where people and activities are found on Earth and why they are found there. This first chapter introduces the basic concepts that geographers use to answer these questions. These include mapping, place, region, scale, space, and connections.

Geography can be divided into two major fields—human geography and physical geography. Physical geography is the study of the physical features and processes on Earth's surface. The Advanced Placement Human Geography course cannot completely ignore physical geography because the two are integrally connected. For example physical geography influences agricultural decisions, migration patterns, as well as housing choices. Human geography is the scientific study of the **location** of people and activities on Earth's surface. It is the study of **where** and **why** human activities are located where they are. Geographers look at the world from a **spatial perspective,** and will study how people and objects vary across Earth's surface. They will also study the relationship or **spatial interaction** between people and objects, as well as the movement or **diffusion** of people and ideas.

Scale is one of the most important concepts for human geographers because it can change one's perceptions of a place depending on which scale you are looking at it through**.** To visualize this concept you might think of the zoom tool on your phone's map program. If you zoom in you see things in great detail, while zooming out gives you a "big picture" idea of a place. Geographers observe a tension between **local diversity** and **globalization.** This approach will help students understand many of the world's problems studied in this course, including those related to political conflicts, development and economic geography, and the environment.

The earliest geographers studied places mainly because of the necessities of trade routes and navigation. The **maps** made by Chinese, Greek, and North African scholars became the foundation of the art and science of mapmaking or **cartography.** The ancient Greek scholar Eratosthenes invented the word geography during the third century B.C.; *geo* means "Earth," and *graphy* means "to write." He also accepted the findings of Aristotle and Plato that the planet was round. Ptolemy, known as the father of cartography, published numerous maps in his eight-volume *Guide to Geography*. After Ptolemy's time (A.D. 100–170), mapmaking became more like a form of artistic expression in Europe and little new exploration came about during this time. However, geographic inquiry continued in other parts of the world. In China, Pei Xiu (the father of Chinese cartography) produced a map of China that used a grid system and graduated scale. It is through the works of Muhammad al-Idrisi and later through the travels of Ibn Battuta that the Islamic world flourished in cartography. European explorers such as the Vikings, Bartholomeu Dias, Christopher Columbus, Vasco Nunez de Balboa, and Ferdinand Magellan mapped the world beyond their continent.

Geography as a discipline developed from description to explanation and analysis. The philosopher Immanuel Kant had placed geography within an overall framework of scientific knowledge by arguing for logical or physical classification. He waned to know where something was located and why it was there. In the eighteenth century Alexander von Humboldt and Carl Ritter argued for **environmental determinism,** the belief that the environment causes human development.

Later geographers argued that landscapes are the products of complex human-environment relationships. This approach is known as **cultural ecology** or **possibilism**. This approach to the subject recognizes that the physical environment may limit certain human activities, but also that people can adapt to their environment.

The **regional** (or **cultural landscape) studies** approach, which emphasizes the unique characteristics of each place, both human and physical, is a third approach to the study of geography. It was pioneered in the late nineteenth and early twentieth centuries by Paul Vidal de la Blache, Jean Brunhes, Carl Sauer and Robert Piatt. While the environmental determinist approach has largely been abandoned by modern geographers, the human-environmental relationships and regional studies approaches remain integral to the scientific study of geography today.

Location and Place

The exact location or **absolute location** of a place on Earth's surface can be pinpointed on a standard grid or **coordinate system**. This universally accepted system of **latitude** and **longitude** consists of imaginary arcs on a globe. Lines of longitude or **meridians** are drawn between the North and South Poles according to a numbering system. 0° is the **prime meridian,** which passes through the Royal Observatory at Greenwich, Great Britain. The meridian on the opposite side of the globe is 180° longitude and is called the **International Date Line.** Lines of latitude or **parallels** are circles drawn around the globe parallel to the **equator**. The grid system is especially useful for determining location where there has been no human settlement.

A **place** is the description of a specific point on Earth's surface; it includes the human and physical features that make it unique. When most people are going on vacation, this is what they subliminally think of: What is the place like? What will I do there? What will the weather be like? All of these questions help to explain a place's unique characteristics. Geographers identify the location of places on Earth in one of four ways—place-names, site, situation, and absolute location. All inhabited places on Earth's surface have been given place-names or **toponyms**. Place-names may tell us about historical origins, such as "Battle" in southern England which is named for the Battle of Hastings. They can also give us an indication of the physical environment such as Aberystwyth in Wales, which means "mouth of the River Ystwyth." Place names may speak to religion, such as Islamabad, Pakistan, or economics such as Gold Point, Nevada. Place-names also change because of political turmoil. The city that was Leningrad in Russia during the Communist era has now been changed back to St. Petersburg.

Site refers to the specific physical characteristics of a place. Site factors such as hilltop, river, and island locations have been important in the historical origins of settlements. The site of Singapore, for example, is a small, swampy island near to the southern tip of the Malay Peninsula. These characteristics can be modified to a certain extent by humans.

Situation or **relative location** describes a place's relationship relative to other places around it. Singapore's relative location near the Strait of Malacca, which is a major passageway between the South China Sea and the Indian Ocean, has been key to its success as a major internationally connected port city.

Last, the exact location or **absolute location** of a place on Earth's surface can be pinpointed and gives us our global address. Through elaborate contemporary mapping using *mashups*, geographers can see the unique characteristics that are at each point on the grid.

Space and Pattern

Distribution refers to the spatial arrangement of something across Earth's surface. The three main properties of distribution are density, concentration, and pattern. **Density** is the frequency with which something occurs in an area. The density of anything could be measured, but in the context of human geography it is usually population. The way in which a feature is spread over an area is its **concentration.** Objects that are closer together are **clustered** and those which are further apart are **dispersed.** Again, geographers usually use the concept of concentration in the context of population. **Pattern** is the geometric arrangement of objects which could be regular or irregular. For example geographers could describe the regular pattern of streets in American and Canadian cities as a grid pattern.

Scale

Map **scale** refers to the ratio between the distance on a map and the actual distance on Earth's surface. Scale is usually presented by cartographers as a fraction (1/24,000), a ratio (1:24,000), a written statement ("1 inch equals 1 mile"), or a graphic scale (_____ equals 1 mile). In a **small-scale** map, the ratio between maps units and ground units is small (such as 1:100,000) and since one map unit equals so many of the same units on the ground, these maps tend to cover large regions (such as a map of the United States). In a **large-scale** map, the ratio between map units and ground units is large (such as 1:5,000) and thus cover much smaller regions (such as a map of a city). Many people confuse these two scales; remember that a **small-scale map** shows a large area without much detail, where a **large-scale map** shows a small area in great detail.

Projection

A map can be used as a **reference tool**, to learn where something is found and to navigate from one place to another. Maps can also be used as a **communication tool**, to depict the location of human activities and physical features, as well as to explain their distribution. Globes are relatively impractical for these uses; thus most maps are flat. The scientific method of transferring the Earth to a flat map is called a **projection**, and inevitably involves some distortion. The things that are commonly distorted on maps usually involve one or more of the following: the shape of an area is distorted, the distance between two areas is incorrect, the relative size of an area appears larger or smaller than it really is, and the direction of a place relative to another can be misleading. There are three general classes of map projections: **conic, cylindrical,** and **planar** (or **azimuthal**) as well as a fourth, a false cylindrical class with an **oval** shape.

Most of the world maps in Rubenstein's text are **equal area projections** because the relative size of an area is kept the same although shapes are distorted. **Conformal maps** distort area but not shape. The uninterrupted **Robinson projection** allocates space to oceans but shows land areas much smaller than on interrupted maps of the same size. The **Mercator projection** minimizes the distortion of shape and direction but grossly distorts area toward the poles, making high latitude places look much larger than they actually are. The interrupted **Goode Homolosine Projection**, often referred to as the "orange peel map," is good at mapping human phenomena across space.

Important technologies related to geography that have been developed since the 1970s include **remote sensing,** the **Global Positioning System (GPS),** and **Geographical Information Systems (GIS).** Remote sensing is the process of acquiring data about Earth's surface from satellites. This could include the mapping of vegetation, winter ice, or changes in weather patterns or deforestation. A GPS device enables one to determine absolute location through an integrated network of satellites. It also allows geographers to determine distances between two points and is thus a valuable navigational tool. GIS enables geographers to map, analyze, and process different pieces of information about a location. These **thematic layers** could include various physical features, transportation infrastructure, population and settlement patterns, and could be analyzed individually or together. Indeed GIS is especially useful when relationships can be seen between the different layers. This is a more sophisticated and technological version of a **thematic map** such as a **choropleth map** (a color coded map used to show the distribution of a geographic phenomena over space).

Key Issues Revisited

1.1. How do geographers describe where things are?

- Geographers use maps to display the location of objects and to get information about places

- Early geographers drew maps of the Earth based on exploration and observation

- GIS and other contemporary technological tools help geographers to understand what they see on Earth's surface

Review Questions

1.1.1. The most important tool to help geographer think spatially is a

A. census.

B. map.

C. stick model.

D. satellite.

E. survey.

1.1.2. He created maps based on information collected from merchants and soldiers:

A. Pei Xiu

B. Ibn Battuta

C. Ptolemy

D. Eratosthenes

E. Columbus

KEY ISSUE 2

Why Is Each Point on Earth Unique?

Learning Outcome 1.2.1: Identify geographic characteristics of places, including toponym, site, and situation.

Location is the position something occupies on Earth. Geographers identify a place's location using place names, site, and situation.

Learning Outcome 1.2.2: Identify the three types of regions.

A formal region is an area within which everyone shares distinctive characteristics. A functional region is an area organized around a node. A vernacular region is an area that people believe exists.

Learning Outcome 1.2.3: Describe two geographic definitions of culture.

Culture can refer to cultural values such as language and religion, or to material culture such as food, clothing, and shelter.

A **region** is generally defined as an area larger than a single city that contains unifying cultural and/or physical characteristics. Regions are sometimes referred to as a "world within a world" because geographers are trying to categorize and make sense of a large area, thus they are looking for common characteristics found within each. The concept is controversial because geographers will debate what exactly makes a region. However it is important as a basic unit of geographic research and a necessary simplification of the world for geographic examination. Geographers have identified three types of regions: formal, functional, and vernacular.

A **formal region** is also called a **uniform region** or a **homogeneous region** because it has specific characteristics that are fairly uniform throughout that region. For example South Korea is a political region, easily identified on a map and also with a very homogenous culture, Korean. The Rocky Mountains constitute a physical region stretching through the United States and Canada. North Africa and the Middle East constitute a formal region characterized by a desert climate as well as an Arab/Islamic culture.

A **functional region** is also called a **nodal region** because it is defined by a social or economic function that occurs between a node or focal point and the surrounding areas. For example the circulation area of the *New York Times* is a functional region and New York is the node.

A **vernacular region** or **perceptual region** is one that exists in people's minds such as the American "South." When individuals are asked to draw a boundary around this region, their boundary will probably be based on stereotypes they associate with the South such as climate, accent, cuisine, and religious practices such as Southern Baptist. It would be difficult to determine the precise boundary of the South. One's attachment to a region perceived as home is sometimes called a **sense of place**. Sometimes people can identify their perceptual region by envisioning or drawing a **mental map**. A mental map is an internal representation of a place on Earth's surface.

Key Issues Revisited

1.2. Why is each point on Earth unique?

- Every place in the world has a unique location on Earth's surface

- Geographers identify regions as areas distinguished by a distinctive combination of cultural, economic, and environmental features which helps us to understand why every region and place is unique

Review Questions

1.2.1. When giving directions to a person, if we say "my house is down past the firehouse" we are describing

A. site.

B. distance.

C. situation.

D. toponym.

E. absolute location.

1.2.2. A mental map is a good way to represent what type of region?

A. formal region

B. functional region

C. vernacular region

D. economic region

E. political region

KEY ISSUE 3

Why Are Different Places Similar?

Learning Outcome 1.3.1: Give examples of changes in economy and culture occurring at global and local scales.

Globalization means that the scale of the world is shrinking in terms of economy and culture.

Learning Outcome 1.3.2: Identify the three properties of distribution across space.

Density is the frequency with which something occurs, concentration is the extent of spread, and pattern is the geometric arrangement.

Learning Outcome 1.3.3: Describe different ways in which geographers approach aspects of cultural identity such as gender, ethnicity, and sexuality.

Males and females, whites and minorities, heterosexuals and homosexuals occupy different places and move across space differently.

Critical geographers have developed different approaches to studying how different cultural groups perceive, experience, organize, and move through space.

Learning Outcome 1.3.4: Describe how characteristics can spread across space over time through diffusion.

Something originates at a hearth and diffuses through either relocation diffusion (physical movement) or expansion diffusion (additive processes).

Learning Outcome 1.3.5: Explain how places are connected through networks and how inequality can hinder connections.

Electronic communications have removed many physical barriers to interaction for those with access to them.

Spatial interaction and interdependence have become increasingly important concepts in geography because of **globalization**, which is the process through which the world is becoming interdependent on a global scale to the extent that smaller scales are becoming less important. It produces a more uniform world. Some might argue that through globalization we are entering a monoculture, where everyone eats at McDonald's, wears the same brand of jeans, and speaks the same language. Globalization ties the world together.

Economic globalization has led to an increase in **transnational corporations** (sometimes called multinational corporations) that invest and operate in many countries. Modern communication and transportation systems have made it much easier to move economic assets around the world. Economically some places are more connected than others because they can supply specialized goods or services within their location. **Complementarity** is the degree to which one place can supply something that another place needs. The concept of **intervening opportunities** also helps to explain connectivity. It is the idea that if one place has a demand for something and there are two potential suppliers, the closer supplier will represent an intervening opportunity because transportation costs will be less. Thus **accessibility** is an important factor in costs and interaction between places. **Transferability** refers to the costs involved in moving goods from one place to another.

There will generally be more interaction between things that are closer than those that are further away. This is **Tobler's First Law of Geography** or the **friction of distance**. Contact will diminish with increasing distance until it ultimately disappears. This is called **distance decay**.

As a result of globalization, there are now greater communications between distant places. **Time-space compression** describes the reduction in time that it takes to diffuse something to a distant place. Think about an Internet video that goes viral or a text message you receive from a friend studying abroad— these illustrate time-space compression in today's world.

Spatial diffusion describes the way that phenomena, such as technological ideas, cultural innovations, disease, or economic goods travel over space. The place from which an innovation originates and diffuses is called a **hearth**. **Relocation diffusion** or **migration diffusion** refers to the physical movement of people from one place to another. It will be discussed later in the context of migration.

Expansion diffusion is the spread of something in a snowballing process. There are three types of expansion diffusion. **Hierarchical diffusion** is the spread of an idea from one node of power and authority to another. For example trends in music, fashion, and art are more likely to diffuse hierarchically from one key city to another (such as from New York to Los Angeles). **Contagious diffusion** is the rapid and widespread diffusion of something throughout a population because of proximity, such as a contagious disease like influenza. **Stimulus diffusion** is the spread of a principle rather than a specific characteristic, such as the certain features of an iPad that are now common on competitors' products.

Key Issues Revisited

1.3. Why are different places similar?

- Geographers work at all scales, from local to global, and the global scale is becoming increasingly important because few places in today's world are completely isolated

- Places display similarities because they are connected to each other

- Geographers study the interactions of people and human activities across space, and they identify the different processes by which people and ideas diffuse from one place to another over time

Review Questions

1.3.1. Globalization means that the scale of the world is

A. increasing.

B. not affected.

C. shrinking.

D. status quo.

E. the same.

1.3.2. The extent of a feature's spread over space is

A. density.

B. distribution.

C. concentration.

D. area.

E. conformity.

KEY ISSUE 4

Why Are Some Human Actions Not Sustainable?

Learning Outcome 1.4.1: Describe the three pillars of sustainability.

Sustainability is the use of Earth's natural resources in ways that ensure availability in the future. This is accomplished through a combination of environmental, economic, and social action.

Learning Outcome 1.4.2: Describe the three abiotic physical systems.

Earth comprises four physical systems: the atmosphere, hydrosphere, lithosphere, and biosphere.

Learning Outcome 1.4.3: Explain how the biosphere interacts with Earth's abiotic systems.

An ecosystem comprises a group of living organisms in the biosphere and their interaction with the atmosphere, lithosphere, and biosphere.

Learning Outcome 1.4.4: Compare ecosystems in the Netherlands and southern Louisiana.

The Dutch have modified the ecosystem of their land in a more sustainable manner than has been the case in southern Louisiana.

Human geographers must focus on the relationship between the physical environment and the humans that live there. Most human geographers focus on the concept of **sustainability**, using Earth's resources (**both renewable and nonrenewable**) in ways that ensure their availability for future generations. The United Nations recognizes the need for **sustainable development** and has embraced the idea of bridging together the environment, the economy, and society.

Through environmental notions, such as **conservation and alternative resources**, the environment will be sustained for future generations to use. The marketplace is where geographers believe that with new technologies we may be able to extract substances that are out of our reach today. The global economy will adjust with the market for natural resources and will allow resources to be more affordable to the majority of people in the world. Although all humans need food, shelter, and clothing, the choices consumers make will aid in sustainable development. If people choose recycled items, or clothes made of natural products, their choices might slow down the resource depletion that is currently happening due to consumerism around the globe.

Geographers focus on the physical systems of Earth: atmosphere, hydrosphere, lithosphere, and biosphere, however, in terms of sustainability the biosphere becomes a focal point. Human activity is now the most important agent of change on the Earth. **Erosion and soil depletion** become exacerbated by human activity. Natural disasters today seem to affect more people due to human activity, such as the breach of the levees in New Orleans during Hurricane Katrina, or the tidal erosion that has taken place due to Superstorm Sandy. Today, more than ever geographers are focusing much of their attention on the long-term affects of human activity on the environment.

Key Issues Revisited

1.4. Why are some human actions not sustainable?

- Geographers are concerned with human interaction on Earth, especially with regard to sustainability

- Geographers believe that you must look at the merging of the environment, the economy, and society to achieve sustainable development

- Human actions on Earth have, in many cases, led to most of the environmental degradation that we now see on Earth

Review Questions

1.4.1. All living systems on Earth would be found in the

A. lithosphere.

B. atmosphere.

C. hydrosphere.

D. biosphere.

E. climosphere.

1.4.2. The belief that the environment causes social development is known as

A. psychology.

B. ecology.

C. environmental determinism.

D. possibilism.

E. sustainability.

Key Terms

Absolute location
Accessibility
Alternative resources
Cartography
Choropleth map
Clustered
Complementarity
Concentration
Conformal maps
Conservation
Contagious diffusion
Coordinate system
Cultural Ecology
Density
Diffusion
Dispersed
Distance decay
Distribution
Environmental determinism
Equal area projection
Equator
Erosion
Expansion diffusion
Formal region
Friction of distance
Functional region
Geographic Information Systems (GIS)
Global Positioning System (GPS)
Globalization
Globalizing forces
Goode Homolosine Projection
Hearth
Hierarchical diffusion
Homogeneous region
International date line
Interrupted map
Intervening opportunities
Large-scale map
Latitude
Local diversity
Location
Longitude
Map

Map as a communication tool
Map as a reference tool
Map projection
Mercator projection
Meridians
Migration diffusion
Nodal region
Nonrenewable resource
Parallels
Pattern
Perceptual region
Place
Possibilism
Prime meridian
Region
Regional (cultural) landscape
Relative location
Relocation diffusion
Remote sensing
Renewable resource
Robinson projection
Scale
Sense of place
Site
Situation
Small-scale map
Soil depletion
Space
Spatial association
Spatial diffusion
Spatial interaction
Spatial perspective
Stimulus diffusion
Sustainability
Thematic layers
Thematic map
Time-space compression
Tobler's First Law of Geography
Toponyms
Transferability
Transnational corporations
Uniform region
Uninterrupted map
Vernacular region

Think Like a Geographer Activities

-Mapping is a very important tool for geographers. Map scale is particularly important in helping see the connections from place to place. Go to: http://www.politico.com/2012-election/map/#/President/2012/ and click on Texas, then Colorado. If you look at the state, then click on the state to look at the county scale; what observation can you make?

-Spatial phenomena are another thing geographers like to look at. Are there connections with places that have unique phenomena occurring even if they are miles away from each other? Can you identify such a phenomenon and make a connection with other places it is occurring? Let's try. Go to http://www.cdc.gov/dhdsp/maps/national_maps/ look at the maps on this site dealing with heart disease and strokes among adults in America. Now search for maps showing fast food restaurants in the United States and obesity rates; explain if there appears to be a correlation. Do your maps look similar for these phenomena?

Quick Quiz

1.1. What is a geographer's most important tool for thinking spatially?
A. remote sensing
B. global positioning satellites
C. globes
D. mashups
E. maps

1.2. A toponym is
A. a physical characteristic of a place.
B. the location of a place in relationship to another place.
C. a name given to a place on Earth.
D. the characteristics that make a place distinct.
E. mathematical grid used to find a place.

1.3. Functional or nodal regions are now being broken down because of
A. redistricting.
B. redlining.
C. technology.
D. blockbusting.
E. culture.

1.4. Spatial association requires geographers to look at the distribution of phenomena
A. on a national, state and urban (local) scale.
B. only on a national scale.
C. only at a state scale.
D. at a global scale.
E. on a global and national scale only.

1.5. A transnational corporation
A. conducts research.
B. operates factories.
C. sells products.
D. does business in many nations.
E. All of these are correct.

1.6. The pillars of sustainability include
A. things that are non-tangible and are only hoped for .
B. creating laws with rigid consequences.
C. bringing together environmental protection, economic growth, and social equity.
D. education for all children.
E. equal access to clean water.

Free Response

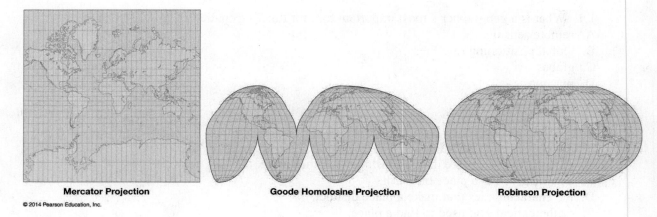

Mercator Projection   Goode Homolosine Projection   Robinson Projection

© 2014 Pearson Education, Inc.

Figure 1-1 Projection

Transferring the locations on Earth's surface is called projection. The problem with projecting a round sphere to a flat plane is that it causes distortion.

A. Describe the four types of distortion.
B. For each type of distortion explain which type of map projection you would use to minimize the distortion.

On the Web

Here are some useful websites for this chapter:

http://www.masteringgeography.com
http://www.nationalgeographic.com
http://www.worldatlas.com
http://www.google.com/mapmaker
http://www.google.com/earth/index.html

Key Figures

Reference the following figures from Chapter 1 in your textbook in order to help you study and prepare for your exam.

Figure 1-9: Projection
Figure 1-10: Geographic Grid
Figure 1-21: Spatial Association
Figure 1-39: Climate Regions
Figure 1-41: Topographic Map

Chapter

2 Population and Health

Where Is the World's Population Distributed?

This chapter describes **population distribution,** the spatial distribution of people on Earth's surface, and where population is growing. The chapter then explains why population is growing at different rates in different places. It discusses the extent to which certain regions of the world may be facing an overpopulation problem.

> **Learning Outcome 2.1.1:** Describe regions where population is clustered and where it is sparse.
>
> Two-thirds of the world's people live in four clusters—East Asia, South Asia, Europe, and Southeast Asia.
>
> **Learning Outcome 2.1.2:** Define three types of density used in population geography.
>
> Arithmetic density is used to describe where people live in the world. Physiological density compares population to resources. Agricultural density measures economic efficiency of food production.

The study of population geography or **demography** is very important because there are more than seven billion people alive today, the growth of the world's population has been most rapid in the last century, and the fastest growth today is in the developing world. Population related issues are key to other chapters especially development, agriculture, and urbanization.

Where are all of these people? Two-thirds of the world's population is clustered in four regions—East Asia, South Asia, Europe, and Southeast Asia. The clustering of the world's population can be shown on a **cartogram**, which depicts the size of countries according to population rather than land area (Figure 2.2 in your textbook). Approximately two-thirds of the world's population lives within 500 kilometers of an ocean. China and India each have over a billion people and together hold over one-third of the world's population. The largest percentages of people in Asia live in rural areas, whereas three-quarters of all Europeans live in towns and cities.

The above overview of world population is at a global level and thus necessarily generalized. The analysis of population patterns at different scales, including continental, national, state, or provincial, and local will reveal different trends and patterns.

The harsh physical environments of Earth's surface, including deserts, tropical rainforests, mountain, and polar regions, are understandably sparsely populated. The portion of the Earth's surface occupied by permanent human settlement is called the **ecumene**.

Arithmetic density (also called **population density)** is a misleading measure of the distribution of people because it is the total number of people divided by the total land area. For example to say that the arithmetic population density of Egypt is 80 people per square kilometer hides the fact that the vast majority of that country's population live in the delta and valley of the Nile River, and much of the country is virtually uninhabited.

Physiological density is a more useful measure of population because it is the number of people supported by a unit area of arable land. The physiological population density of Egypt is 2,296 people per square kilometer, which is a very good measure of the pressure on agricultural land in that country.

Agricultural density is the ratio of the number of farmers to the amount of agricultural land. Countries like Canada and the United States have much lower agricultural densities than less developed countries like India and Bangladesh. In more developed countries technology related to agriculture allow a few farmers to work huge area of land and feed many people. Thus agricultural density and physiological density are good measures of the relationship between population and resources together with the level of development in a country.

Key Issues Revisited

2.1. Where is the world's population distributed?

- The world's population is concentrated in a few places

- People tend to avoid places that they consider to be too wet, too dry, too cold, or too mountainous

Review Questions

2.1.1. The study of populations is

A. physiography.

B. democracy.

C. demography.

D. ethnography.

E. biology.

2.1.2. Most of the world's population is clustered into these four areas:

A. East Asia, South Asia, Europe, and Southeast Asia.

B. Europe, East Asia, South Asia, and Africa.

C. East Asia, South Asia, Southeast Asia, and Africa.

D. South Asia, Southeast Asia, Europe, and Africa.

E. South Asia, Southeast Asia, East Asia, and Europe.

KEY ISSUE 2

Why Is Global Population Increasing?

Learning Outcome 2.2.1: Understand how to measure population growth through the natural increase rate.

The natural increase rate is the percentage by which a population grows in a year.

Learning Outcome 2.2.2: Understand how to measure births and deaths through CBR and CDR.

The CBR is the total number of live births in a year for every 1,000 people alive. The CDR is the total number of deaths per 1,000 people.

Learning Outcome 2.2.3: Understand how to read a population pyramid.

A population pyramid displays the percentage of population by age and gender. A pyramid with a broad base means a country has a relatively high percentage of young children.

The crude birth rate, crude death rate, and natural increase rate are used to measure population change in a country. The **crude birth rate (CBR)** or **natality rate** and **crude death rate (CDR)** are statistical terms that refer to the total number of live births and deaths respectively per thousand people in a country. Where the CBR is higher than the CDR, **natural increase (NIR)** occurs. This does not account for migration. If the CDR is about the same as the CBR a country has **zero population growth (ZPG).** If the CDR is higher than the CBR, there is a **negative NIR.** The **demographic equation** is the global difference between births and deaths.

During the first decade of the twenty-first century the world rate of natural increase was 1.2%, which meant that the world's population was growing each year by 1.2%. It would take the world 54 years to double its population given this rate of growth; this is called **doubling time.** During the 1960s and 1970s the world's doubling time was about 35 years because the NIR was 2.2%.

It is important to understand there are major regional differences in rates of population growth. The NIR exceeds 2% in many countries in sub-Saharan Africa. Indeed most of the world's population growth is now in developing countries. At the other extreme some Western European countries are now experiencing negative population growth, such as Germany, which has a NIR of –0.2%. China, the most populous country in the world, has done much in terms of government mandates to lower its population growth rates. India will soon surpass China as the most populous country in the world.

The highest crude birth rates are in Africa and the lowest are in Europe and North America. The **total fertility rate (TFR)** is used by demographers to measure the number of births in a country. The TFR is the average number of children a woman will have during her childbearing years (ages 15 through 49). In some cases, like in Nigeria, Uganda, and Angola, the TFR exceeds six.

The **infant mortality rate (IMR)** is the annual number of deaths of infants under one year of age, compared with total live births, and is usually expressed as number of deaths per 1,000 births. IMR is a measure of a country's level of health care, and the highest rates are in less developed countries. The other useful measure of mortality is **life expectancy**. This is the number of years a newborn infant can expect to live at current mortality levels. Life expectancy rates are sometimes twice as high in developed countries than in developing countries, for instance the life expectancy in Lesotho is only 48 years, whereas it is 82 years in France.

The **age-sex distribution (ratio)** of a country's population can be shown on a **population pyramid.** It will show the distribution of a country's population between males and females of various ages. The country's **sex ratio** is the number of males per 100 females. A population pyramid will normally show the percentage of the total population in five-year age groups, with the youngest group at the base of the pyramid and the oldest group at the top. Males are usually shown on the left and females on the right. Each age-sex group is called a population **cohort**. Population pyramids can tell us much about the population history of a country. A pyramid with a wide base shows a rapidly growing country with a large proportion of young people, and is typical of a less developed county. A pyramid that is more rectangular depicts a country with a relatively even number of young, middle-aged, and older people, and is typical of a more developed country. Population pyramids are also useful tools to analyze and predict future population growth. Such a usage is referred to as **population projection**.

The **dependency ratio** is the percentage of people in a population who are either too old (over

65) or young (0–14) to work and thus must be supported by others.

Key Issues Revisited

2.2. Why is global population increasing?

- Most of the world's natural increase is in the LDCs of Africa, Asia, and Latin America

- Most European and North American countries now have low population growth rates, and some are experiencing population decline

- The difference in rates of natural increase between MDCs and LDCs is mainly due to differences in CBRs rather than CDRs

Review Questions

2.2.1. With a NIR of 1.2% the world's population would double in approximately _____ years.

A. 35 years

B. 87 years

C. 54 years

D. 7 years

E. 110 years

2.2.2. The region with the highest TFR is

A. Europe.

B. North Africa.

C. Sub-Saharan Africa.

D. India.

E. China.

KEY ISSUE 3

Why Does Population Growth Vary Among Regions?

Learning Outcome 2.3.1: Describe the four stages of the demographic transition.

Stage 1 has high CBR and CDR and low NIR. In stage 2 the NIR rises because the CDR declines. In stage 3 the NIR moderates because the CBR starts to decline. Stage 4 has low CBR, CDR, and NIR.

Learning Outcome 2.3.2: Summarize two approaches to reducing birth rates.

The CBR can be lowered either through education and health care or through diffusion of contraception.

Learning Outcome 2.3.3: Summarize Malthus's argument about the relationship between population and resources.

Malthus argued in 1798 that population would grow more rapidly than resources. Recent experience shows that the population has not grown as rapidly as Malthus forecast.

Learning Outcome 2.3.4: Summarize the possible stage 5 of the demographic transition.

Japan and some European countries may be in a possible stage 5, characterized by a decline in population, because CDR exceeds CBR.

The **demographic transition model** explains changes in the natural increase rate as a function of economic development. It is a process with four stages, and every country is in one of them.

Stage 1 of the demographic transition is one of high birth rates and death rates and consequently very low growth. Most of human history was spent in stage 1 but no countries remain in that stage today. Stage 2 is one of high growth or **demographic momentum** because death rates decline and birth rates remain high. Demographic momentum will be sustained because of a relatively young population. The demographic transition assumes that countries enter stage 2 because they go through the **industrial revolution.** Technologies associated with industry helped countries to produce more food and improve sanitation and health. Western European countries and North America entered stage 2 after 1750. Countries in Latin America, Asia, and Africa have experienced stage 2 much more recently, and without experiencing an industrial revolution. The rapid increase in population associated with stage 2 is often referred to as a **population explosion.** Developing countries have moved into stage 2 because of a **medical revolution,** the diffusion of medical technologies to LDCs. The sudden decline in death rates that comes from technological innovations has now occurred everywhere.

Countries will move from stage 2 to stage 3 when their crude birth rates drop sharply as a result of changes in social, economic patterns as well as government policies that encourage people to have fewer children. The demographic transition assumes that people in stage 3 are more likely to live in an urban and industrial world with few children. Chile is in stage 3 of the demographic transition. The drop in birth rates that comes with changes in social customs has yet to be achieved in many countries.

Countries will reach stage 4 of the demographic transition because their birth rates will continue to decline until the natural increase rate drops to zero. This is true of countries in Europe together with Canada, Australia, and Japan. The demographic transition assumes that this occurs because of more changes in social customs such as women being educated and then entering the labor force in larger numbers.

It could be argued that some countries, primarily Western and Northern European, that are now experiencing population decline. Very low CBR and an increasing CDR, which leads to a negative NIR, characterize them. These countries will have entered stage 5 of the demographic transition. These countries have a low **elderly support ratio**, which means that there are fewer working age people (15 to 64) than there are old people who depend on pensions, health care, and other government support.

One of the most famous models to explain changes in population over time was developed by Thomas Malthus. Malthus was an English economist and demographer who published *Essay on the Principle of Population* in 1798. He argued that the world's population was growing geometrically or **exponentially**, but food supplies were only growing arithmetically (see figure 2.29 in your textbook). According to Malthus this would lead to "negative checks" consisting of starvation and disease because of a lack of food. The only way to avoid this would be for populations to lower crude birth rates.

Malthus' theory is still potentially relevant today because of rapid population growth in some LDCs. His adherents today are called **neo-Malthusians** and are led by Paul Ehrlich who has made a similar argument to Malthus in *The Population Bomb*. Neo-Malthusians such as Robert Kaplan and Thomas

Fraser Homer-Dixon have broadened Malthus' theory to include fuel, agricultural land, and other resources as well as food.

Malthus has his critics too. The Marxist theorist Friedrich Engels believes that the world has enough resources to eliminate hunger and poverty if they are more equally shared. Contemporary critics include Julian Simon and Esther Boserup who argue that larger populations can actually stimulate economic growth. Malthus was terribly pessimistic and did not foresee the development of new agricultural technologies or the human ability to reduce population growth rates.

Most demographers would agree that some parts of the world are **overpopulated**, where a country can no longer sustainably support its population because it has reached its carrying capacity. In human geography **carrying capacity** refers to the number of people a given area can support.

The CBR has declined rapidly since 1990 except in some countries in sub-Saharan Africa. This has occurred partly as a result of economic development which has resulted in more money for education and health care. Birth rates have also been lowered because of diffusion of modern contraceptives. Some countries, such as Bangladesh, have reduced their birth rates like this without economic development. There is opposition to birth control programs from some countries for religious and political reasons.

Key Issues Revisited

2.3. Why does population growth vary among regions?

- The demographic transition shows the change in a country's population. According to this model a country will move from a situation of high birth and death rates, with little population growth, to one of low birth and death rates, with low population growth

- Through the demographic transition, the total population increases tremendously, because the death rate declines some years before the birth rate does

- The MDCs of Europe and North America have reached stage four of the demographic transition

- African, Asian, and Latin American countries are at stage two or three of the demographic transition, where population growth is rapid, death rates have declined sharply, but birth rates remain relatively high

Review Questions

2.3.1. What caused Stage 2 of the demographic transition model to occur in Africa?

A. Neolithic Revolution

B. Medical Revolution

C. Industrial Revolution

D. Second Agricultural Revolution

E. Genetically Modified Crops

2.3.2. A country with a negative NIR would be

A. Russia.

B. Angola.

C. Guatemala.

D. United States.

E. China.

KEY ISSUE 4

Why Do Some Regions Face Health Threats?

Learning Outcome 2.4.1: Summarize the four stages of the epidemiologic transition.

Stage 1 was characterized by pestilence and famine, stage 2 by pandemics, and stages 3 and 4 by degenerative diseases.

Learning Outcome 2.4.2: Summarize the reasons for a stage 4 and possible stage 5 of the epidemiologic transition.

Evolution, poverty, and increased connections may influence the resurgence of infectious diseases.

Learning Outcome 2.4.3: Describe the diffusion of AIDs.

Learning Outcome 2.4.4: Understand reasons for variations in health care between developed and developing countries.

Health care varies widely around the world because developing countries generally lack resources to provide the same level of health care as developed countries.

Learning Outcome 2.4.5: Understand reasons for variations in health between developed and developing countries.

Medical researchers have identified an **epidemiologic transition** that focuses on the causes of death in each stage of the demographic transition. **Epidemiology** is the branch of medicine that is concerned with disease. In stage 1 of the epidemiologic transition, infectious and parasitic diseases were the main causes of death. These include the Black Plague and cholera **pandemics.** A pandemic occurs over a very wide geographic area unlike an **epidemic**, which is more localized. These causes of death were most common for people in countries in stage 1 and the early part of stage 2 of the demographic transition.

Stage 3 of the epidemiologic transition is associated with degenerative and human-created diseases such as heart diseases and cancer. As LDCs have moved from stage 2 to stage 3 of the demographic transition, the incidence of infectious diseases has declined. Human-created diseases are more typical of countries in stage 4 of the demographic transition.

Some medical researchers have argued that the world is now moving into stage 5 of the epidemiologic transition, characterized by a reemergence of infectious and parasitic diseases. This could be for a number of reasons including the evolution of infectious disease microbes, poverty, and improved travel. Avian flu is one of the "new" infectious diseases that have emerged in recent decades, and it has the potential to become pandemic. However, AIDS is the most lethal epidemic of recent years, especially in sub-Saharan Africa, where there were more than 25 million people infected with HIV in 2005.

Key Issues Revisited

2.4. Why do some regions face health threats?

- As a result of a dramatic decline in the death rate, global population grew at an unprecedented rate during the second half of the twentieth century

- Birth rates began to decline sharply during the 1990s, slowing world population growth and reducing fears of overpopulation in most regions

- Demographers agree that the current rate of natural increase must be further reduced, but they disagree on the methods to achieve this goal

Review Questions

2.4.1. The bubonic plague would occur during what stage of the epidemiologic transition?

A. Stage 5

B. Stage 4

C. Stage 3

D. Stage 2

E. Stage 1

2.4.2. Most of the "new" pandemics are spread through

A. stimulus diffusion.

B. relocation diffusion.

C. hierarchical diffusion.

D. functional diffusion.

E. parasitic diffusion.

Key Terms

Age-sex distribution (ratio)
Agricultural density
Arithmetic density
Carrying capacity
Cartogram
Cohort
Crude birth rate (CBR)
Crude death rate (CDR)
Demographic equation
Demographic momentum
Demographic transition model
Demography
Dependency ratio
Doubling time
Ecumene
Elderly support ratio
Epidemic
Epidemiologic transition
Epidemiology
Exponentially

Industrial Revolution
Infant mortality rate (IMR)
Life expectancy
Medical revolution
Natality rate
Natural increase rate (NIR)
Neo-Malthusian
Overpopulated
Pandemic
Physiological density
Population density
Population distribution
Population explosion
Population projection
Population pyramid
Sex ratio
Thomas Malthus
Total fertility rate (TFR)
Zero population growth (ZPG)

Think Like a Geographer Activities

Go to http://www.worldpopulationatlas.org/ and look at world cartograms. Why do geographers to display population related issues use cartograms?

Go to http://populationpyramid.net/ and look at the population pyramids for Congo, Kuwait, the Russian Federation, and the United States. What similarities or differences do you see? What might account for these?

Quick Quiz: (Matching)

2.1. Total fertility rate   A. Males per 100 females
2.2. Dependency ratio   B. Average number of children women has
2.3. Infant mortality   C. People who are too old or too young to work
2.4. Natural increase rate   D. Number of deaths compared to live births
2.5. Sex ratio   E. Percentage by which population grows annually

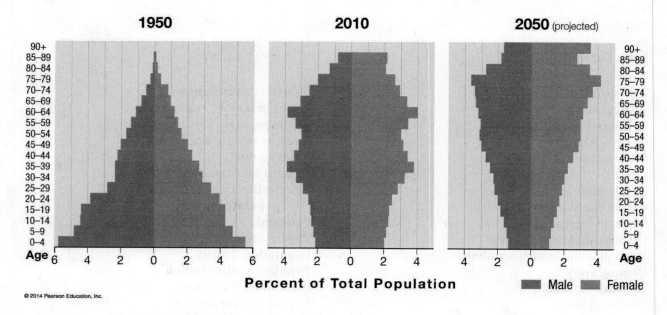

Figure 2.1 Japan's Changing Population Pyramids

Japan's population pyramid has changed dramatically since 1950 and is projected to change even more by 2050.

2.6. Looking at the 1950 pyramid, which stage of the demographic transition model was Japan in?
A. Stage 1
B. Stage 2
C. Stage 3
D. Stage 4
E. Stage 5

2.7. What stage were they in by 2010?
A. Stage 1
B. Stage 2
C. Stage 3
D. Stage 4
E. Stage 5

2.8. By 2050, what will the Japanese government be most concerned with?
A. Crude birth rates
B. Infant mortality rates
C. Radiation from nuclear power plants
D. Elderly support ratio
E. Lack of childcare facilities

Free Response

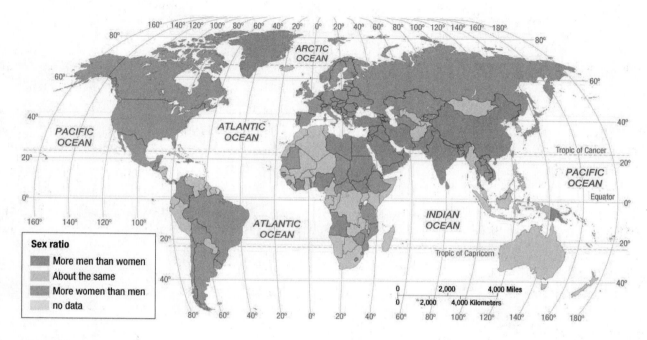

© 2014 Pearson Education, Inc.

Figure 2-2 Sex Ratio

By looking at this map answer the following demographic questions:

A. Identify countries that include more men than women.
B. Describe social, economic, and political factors that could account for these discrepancies.
C. Explain what actions a country might take to alleviate these factors.

On the Web

http://www.masteringgeography.com
http://www.worldpopulationatlas.org
http://populationpyramid.
http://www.prb.org net/

Key Figures

Chapter

3 Migration

Where Are Migrants Distributed?

The chapter focuses on migration, which is a specific type of relocation diffusion. It examines why people move permanently or migrate, both internally and internationally. Migration patterns are analyzed as well as the obstacles faced by migrants.

Learning Outcome 3.1.1: Describe the difference between international and internal migration.

Migration can be international (between countries, either voluntary or forced) or internal (within a country, either interregional or intraregional).

Learning Outcome 3.1.2: Identify the principal sources of immigrants during the three main eras of U.S. immigration.

The United States has had three main eras of immigration. The principal source of immigrants has shifted from Europe during the first two eras to Latin America and Asia during the third (current) era.

At a global scale people generally migrate from the developing to the developed world. The three largest flows are from Asia to Europe and North America, and from Latin America.

More than most other countries, the United States is a land of immigrants. About 75 million people migrated to the United States between 1820 and 2010. There have been three major eras of immigration to the United States. The first era was the original settlement of colonies in the 1600s. The second was from the mid-nineteenth century to the early twentieth century, and the third was from the 1970s until the present. All three eras have involved people coming to the United States from countries that were at stage two of the demographic transition.

Immigration to the American colonies consisted of mostly forced migration from Africa and a mixture of forced and voluntary migration from Europe. There were three peaks of the second era of immigration. The first peak of immigration was during the 1840s and 1850s and consisted of people largely from Western Europe. The second peak was during the late 1800's and again most migrants were from Western Europe, especially Germany and Ireland, although there were increasing numbers of people from Scandinavia. The third peak was from the late 1800s until the early 1900s and consisted of people largely from Southern and Eastern Europe who came to work in the factories of the Industrial Revolution.

Recent immigration to the United States has been from less developed regions, especially Asia and Latin America. The three leading sources of U.S. immigrants from Asia are China, India, and the Philippines. In the 1980s Mexico became the leading source of immigrants to the United States. Although the pattern of immigration to the United States has changed, the reason for immigration remains essentially the same. People are pushed from their homeland by economic and political conditions, and are attracted to the economic and social potential of life in the United States.

Today's immigrants to the United States are clustered in California, New York, Florida, and Texas. New immigrants often move to places where family members and friends from their home country have already migrated. This is called **chain migration**.

Key Issues Revisited

3.1. Where are migrants distributed?

- At a global scale, the largest flows of migrants are from Asia to Europe and from Asia and Latin America to the United States

- The United States receives by far the largest number of migrants

Review Questions

3.1.1. A permanent move from one country to another is

A. interregional migration.

B. internal migration.

C. intraregional migration.

D. tourist migration.

E. international migration.

3.1.2. The largest flow of migrants is from

A. Asia to Europe.

B. Asia to North America.

C. both A & B.

D. Asia to Oceania.

E. Africa to Europe.

KEY ISSUE 2

Why do People Migrate Within a Country?

Learning Outcome 3.2.1: Describe the history of interregional migration in the United States.

Migration within the United States has primarily occurred from east to west, though at varying rates. Recently, interregional migration has also occurred from north to south.

Learning Outcome 3.2.2: Describe interregional migration in Russia and Canada.

The world's two largest countries have distinctive patterns of interregional migration. These patterns derive unequal distribution of population within these countries.

Learning Outcome 3.2.3: Describe interregional migration in China and Brazil.

China and Brazil also have unequal population Chinese have been migrating from the rural interior to the large coastal cities. Brazilians have been encouraged to move from the large coastal cities to the interior.

Learning Outcome 3.2.4: Explain differences among the three forms of intraregional migration.

Three intraregional migration patterns are from rural to urban areas, from urban to suburban areas, and from urban to rural areas.

Historically the most significant migration trend has been **interregional migration** westward in United States to obtain cheap land and potential wealth. The population center of the United States has moved westward and more recently southward. In the 1960s and 1970s large numbers of white, middle-class Americans moved from the older northeastern and midwestern states to the south and the west coast. At this time northern industrial states were known as the **Rust Belt** because their economy was declining as factories closed and people moved. The towns that are left behind are sometimes referred to as the **Hollow Core**. At the same time the south, which had been known as the **Cotton Belt** because of its agricultural poverty, became known as the **Sun Belt,** a land of opportunity. The migration of African-Americans followed a different pattern, from the rural south to large cities in the north. Interregional migration in the United States has not been as significant in the first decade of the twenty-first century, largely because of a narrowing of regional differences in employment opportunities.

Interregional migration has also been important in other countries. Soviet policy encouraged people to move to Russia's Far North to develop industry. It didn't work very well and ended with the collapse of the Soviet Union. Brazil has encouraged people to move into the interior, especially since the building of Brasilia in 1960. The Chinese are also experiencing a mass exodus of people from the interior to large cities on the coast.

Intraregional migration has also been important in many countries. In the United States as well as most MDCs, the most important trend since the middle of the twentieth century has been the move to suburbs from central cities. A new trend in North America and Western Europe has been **counterurbanization**, from urban to rural areas for lifestyle preferences especially now that modern technology allows people to work more easily from their homes.

Migration from rural to urban areas has been very important in LDCs. Worldwide more than 20 million people are estimated to migrate each year from rural to urban areas. People seek economic opportunities with this type of migration and, especially in LDCs, are pushed because of failed agricultural systems.

Key Issues Revisited

3.2. Why do people migrate within a country?

- There is both interregional and intraregional migration within a country

- Historically, interregional migration was important in settling the frontier of large countries such as the United States, Russia, and Brazil

- The most important intraregional trends are from rural to urban areas within LDCs, and from cities to suburbs within MDCs

Review Questions

3.2.1. Historically, the "center of population gravity" in the United States has been moving

A. eastward.

B. north.

C. northeast.

D. westward.

E. southeast.

3.2.2. The government of Brazil encouraged interregional migration by

A. punishing those who refused to move.

B. cleaning out the Favelas.

C. moving the capital.

D. building a transcontinental railroad.

E. setting up a quota system.

KEY ISSUE 3

Why do People Migrate?

Learning Outcome 3.3.1: Provide examples of political, environmental, and economic push and pull factors.

People migrate because of a combination of push and pull factors. These factors may be political, environmental, and economic. Most people migrate for economic push and pull reasons.

Learning Outcome 3.3.2: Summarize the flows of migrant workers in Europe and Asia.

People migrate for temporary work, especially from developing countries to developed countries, where they take jobs that are not desired by local residents.

E.G. Ravenstein, a nineteenth century geographer, identified 11 laws of migration, which can be roughly organized into three main elements: the reasons migrants move, the distance they move, and the major characteristics of migration. Migration is a specific type of relocation diffusion and is a form of **mobility,** a more general term dealing with all types of movement. **Migration** is the movement of a person from one place to another. It can include movement at many different scales, such as short-term, repetitive, or cyclical movements called **circulation,** or **intercontinental migration,** which is from one continent to another. **Emigration** is movement *from* a location whereas **immigration** is movement *to* a location. The difference between the number of immigrants and the number of emigrants is the **net migration.**

People generally migrate because of push and pull factors. **Push factors** include anything that would cause someone to leave their present location, such as the violation of a person's **activity space.** **Pull factors** induce people to move to a new location. Four major kinds of push and pull factors can be identified. These are economic, political, cultural, and environmental.

Economic factors that can lead to migration include job opportunities, cycles of economic growth and recession, and cost of living. The United States and Canada have been important destinations for economic migrants lured by economic pull factors. An example of this is **place utility,** where a place may offer economic incentives in an effort to attract people to their town or city.

Armed conflict and the policies of oppressive regimes have been important political push factors in forcing out those who become refugees. A **refugee,** according to the United Nations, is a person who, "owing to well-founded fear of being persecuted for reasons of race, religion, nationality, membership in a particular social group, or political opinion, is outside the country of his nationality, and is unable to or, owing to such fear, is unwilling to avail himself of the protection of that country." The majority of the world's refugees (2010) have migrated from Afghanistan and Iraq because of the recent wars. There are also a significant number of **internally displaced people (IDP)**, who are forced to migrate but are still within their national borders. The last type of forced migrant is **an asylum seeker**, a person who migrates to another country hoping to be recognized as a refugee. There are also political pull factors such as the promise of political freedom. It has been this factor that has lured so many people from the communist countries of Eastern Europe to Western Europe in the second half of the twentieth century.

Cultural factors can encourage people to move to places where they will be more at home culturally. A good example of a cultural pull factor is the relocation of Jews to the newly formed state of Israel after the Second World War. Israel is the ancestral hearth of Jewish culture and it serves as a place where Jewish people can reestablish social ties and create a sense of political unity.

Environmental pull and push factors are largely related to physical geography. People will be pulled towards physically attractive regions such as the Rocky Mountains and the Mediterranean coast of southern Europe. People might also be pushed from places by floods and droughts. The flooding in New Orleans and other Gulf Coast communities in 2005 following Hurricane Katrina caused around 1,400 deaths and forced several hundred thousand people from their homes. Indeed many people are forced to move by water-related disasters because they live in vulnerable areas, such as a **floodplain**.

Migrants do not always go to their intended destination because of an **intervening obstacle**, which is an environmental or cultural feature that hinders migration. Sometimes a migrant will stop and stay at a place en route to their intended destination because of an **intervening opportunity**, which is an environmental or cultural feature that favors migration.

According to Ravenstein, most migrants move only a short distance and within a country. **Internal migration** is permanent movement within a country. This is the most common type of movement and is consistent with the principles of distance decay. **Interregional migration** is one type of internal migration, and is movement from one region of a country to another. Historically this has usually been from rural to urban, but developed countries are now experiencing more urban to rural migration. The other type of internal migration is **intraregional migration**, movement within a region. In the developed world this has largely been urban to suburban but these patterns are now beginning to change.

One of Ravenstein's laws states that long-distance migrants to other countries usually relocate to major economic and urban centers. The permanent migration from one country to another is **international migration**, and it can be voluntary or forced. **Voluntary migration** is when someone chooses to leave a place as a result of push or pull factors. **Forced migration** is when someone is moved from their home without any choice.

A century ago Ravenstein stated that most long-distance migrants were male adults rather than families with children. Today there are much larger numbers of females migrating internationally together with their children, especially from Mexico to the United States. This is a reflection of the changing role of women. Much of the migration from Mexico to the United States is illegal and seasonal.

The demographer Wilbur Zelinsky has identified a **migration transition**, which outlines changes in the migration pattern in a society during different stages of the demographic transition. According to the migration transition, international migration usually occurs when countries are in stage two of the demographic transition. For example, international migrants moved from Western Europe to the United States as a result of the technological changes related to the Industrial Revolution. Internal migration becomes more important when countries are in stages three and four of the demographic transition. According to migration transition theory, people generally move from cities to suburbs during these stages. Zelinsky theorizes that countries in stages three and four of the demographic transition are the destinations of international migrants leaving stage two counties because of economic push and pull factors.

Key Issues Revisited

3.3. Why do people migrate?

- Push factors include emigration from a location for political, economic, and environmental reasons

- Pull factors include immigration for political, economic, and environmental factors

- We can distinguish between international and internal migration

Review Questions

3.3.1. According to E. G. Ravenstein the most common reason people migrate is for

A. political reasons.

B. environmental reasons.

C. war.

D. authoritarian reasons.

E. economic reasons.

3.3.2. Most immigrants in Europe who are in search of work come from

A. Poland.

B. Egypt.

C. Spain.

D. Portugal.

E. Italy.

KEY ISSUE 4

Why Do Migrants Face Obstacles?

Learning Outcome 3.4.1: Identify the types of immigrants who are given preference to enter the United States.

Immigration is tightly controlled by most countries. The United States gives preference to immigrants with family members already in the country and to those who have special job skills.

Learning Outcome 3.4.2: Describe the population characteristics of unauthorized immigrants to the United States.

The United States has more than 11 million unauthorized immigrants, who are in the country without proper documents. Most have emigrated from Mexico.

Learning Outcome 3.4.3: Describe characteristics of immigrants to the United States.

In the past, most immigrants were males, but now an increasing share of immigrants to the United States are women and children.

Learning Outcome 3.4.4: Compare American and European attitudes toward immigrants.

Americans and Europeans have divided and ambivalent attitudes toward the large number of immigrants, especially those arriving without proper documentation.

The United States uses a quota system to limit the number of foreign citizens who can migrate permanently to the country. **Quotas** are maximum limits on the number of people who can immigrate to the United States from one country during a one-year period. Initial quota laws were designed to allow more Europeans to come to the United States, rather than Asians. Quotas for individual countries were eliminated in 1968 and replaced with hemisphere quotas. In 1978 the hemisphere quotas were replaced by a global quota, which was set at 700,000 in 1990. The majority of legal immigration today is chain migration. Some preference is also given to skilled workers, which leads to **brain drain**, the emigration of talented people. According to the World Bank in 2012, 8 out of 10 Haitians with a college degree lived abroad.

There have been increasing numbers of illegal, **unauthorized,** or **undocumented immigrants** to the United States. In 2010 the Urban Institute estimated that there might have been as many as 11.2 million undocumented immigrants, including about 58% from Mexico. It is a controversial topic because although undocumented immigrants take jobs that few others want, most Americans would also like more effective border patrols. Thus some favor **amnesty** for illegal immigrants whereas others believe that they should be deported.

Europe allows temporary **guest workers** to legally work for at least minimum wages in their countries. They serve the same purpose as the vast majority of illegal immigrants in the United States. Luxembourg and Switzerland have especially high percentages of foreign-born workers in their labor force. Between 1999 and 2008, the foreign-born population in Spain rose from around $^3/_4$ million to $\mathbf{5^1/_4}$ million.

In the nineteenth century, **time-contract** workers migrated to work in mines and on plantations for a set period of time, although many of them stayed. More than 33 million ethnic Chinese currently live in other countries. Thus it is sometimes difficult to distinguish between economic migrants and refugees.

The United States has generally regarded emigrants from Cuba as political refugees since Castro's 1959 revolution. Economic and political refugees from Haiti have not been quite as welcome in the United States. Vietnamese boat people were regarded as political refugees after the Vietnam War, when thousands fled the war-ravaged country. Vietnam remains an important source of immigrants to the United States today, but largely because of the pull of economic opportunity rather than the push of political persecution.

Immigrants often face opposition from some citizens of host countries because they are often culturally, ethnically, and religiously different. For example there have been open ethnic and racial conflicts between citizens and migrants in Western Europe and Australia in the first decade of the twenty-first century.

Key Issues Revisited

3.4. Why do migrants face obstacles?

- Migrants have difficulty getting permission to enter other countries, and often face hostility from local citizens once they arrive

- Immigration laws restrict the number who can legally enter the United States

- Guest workers migrate temporarily to perform menial jobs in Europe and the Middle East

Review Questions

3.4.1. Congressional preferences for people wishing to immigrate to the United States include all of these **except**

A. family reunification.

B. skilled workers.

C. ethnic diversification.

D. refugees.

E. professionals.

3.4.2. Many localities have passed resolutions to help unauthorized immigrants, this movement is called

A. sanctuary city.

b. illegal interference.

c. federalism.

d. egalitarianism.

e. civil disobedience.

Key Terms

Activity space
Amnesty
Asylum Seeker
Brain drain
Chain migration
Circulation
Cotton Belt
Counterurbanization
Emigration
Floodplain
Forced migration
Guest workers
Hollow Core
Immigration
Intercontinental migration
Internally displaced people (IDP)
Internal migration
International migration
Interregional migration

Intervening obstacle
Intervening opportunity
Intraregional migration
Migration
Migration transition
Mobility
Net migration
Place utility
Pull factors
Push factors
Quotas
Refugees
Rust Belt
Sun Belt
Time-contract workers
Unauthorized immigrants
Undocumented immigration
Voluntary migration

Think Like a Geographer Activities

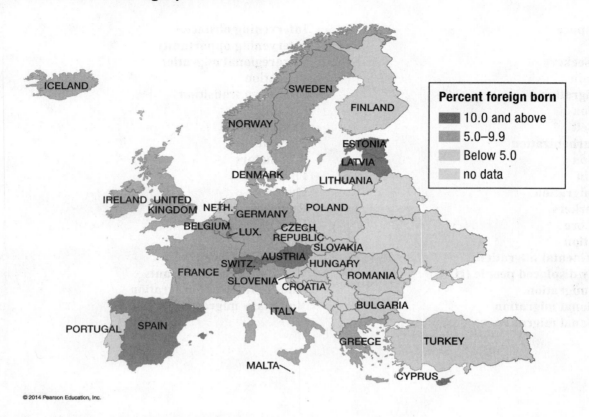

© 2014 Pearson Education, Inc.

Figure 3-1 Percentage of Immigrants in Europe

A. What are some social/cultural issues that occur in countries like Spain, Estonia, or Latvia?
B. Describe potential actions by the government to deal with these issues.

Quick Quiz Matching

3.1. net migration	A.	change in migration due to social/economic changes
3.2. asylum seeker	B.	forced to migrate within their country for political reasons
3.3. internally displaced person	C.	hope of economic opportunity
3.4. pull factor	D.	an ocean, a desert
3.5. refugees	E.	difference between in migration and out migration
3.6. chain migration	F.	migrant to another country hoping to be called a refugee
3.7. intervening obstacle	G.	forced to migrate across country borders
3.8. migration transition	H.	migrating to join family members

Free Response

Countries with large land areas have distinctive patterns of interregional migration.

A. Determine two countries that experience interregional migration.
B. Identify one characteristic of migrants that each country shares.
C. Discuss one outcome occurring in both countries due to interregional migration.

On the Web

http://www.masteringgeography.com
http://www.nationmaster.com/graph/imm_imm_pop_num_of_imm-immigration-immigrant-population-number-immigrants
http://unstats.un.org/unsd/demographic/sconcerns/migration/
http://www.oecd.org/migration/internationalmigrationoutlook2011.htm
http://web.worldbank.org

Key Figures

Table 3-1 Comparison of Demographic Transition and Migration Transition
Figure 3-6 Global Migration Patterns
Figure 3-10 Changing Center of U. S. Population
Figure 3-25 Political Factors: Refugees and IDPS

Chapter

4 Folk and Popular Culture

Where Are Folk and Popular Leisure Activities Distributed?

Rubenstein defines culture as the body of customary beliefs, social forms, and material traits that together constitute a group of people's distinct tradition. Culture can be distinguished from habit and custom. A **habit** is a repetitive act that an individual performs, and a **custom** is a repetitive act of a group. Culture combines three things—values, material artifacts, and political institutions. This chapter deals with the material artifacts of culture or **material culture**, which includes the **built environment** or visible objects that a group possesses and leaves behind for the future. It will focus on the two basic categories, folk and popular culture, their origins, diffusion, and spatial distribution. Popular culture has a more widespread distribution than folk culture, and its globalization causes problems that are addressed here.

Learning Outcome 4.1.1: Compare the origin, diffusion, and distribution of folk and popular culture.

Folk culture is more likely to have an anonymous origin and to diffuse slowly through migration, whereas popular culture is more likely to be invented and diffuse rapidly with the use of modern communications.

Learning Outcome 4.1.2: Compare the characteristics of folk and popular music.

Popular music has wide global distribution because of connections among artists and styles.

Learning Outcome 4.1.3: Describe how sports have been transformed from folk to popular culture.

Sports that originated as isolated folk customs have been organized into popular culture with global distribution.

Folk culture refers to the cultural practices of small, homogeneous groups living in traditional societies. Folk cultures are usually isolated and rural, with subsistence economies. Distinctive architecture and other material artifacts such as tools, musical instruments, and clothing contribute to the uniqueness of folk cultures. Nonmaterial aspects of folk culture include songs **(folk songs)**, stories **(folklore)**, and belief systems. Folk cultures originate in multiple **hearths** because of their isolation.

Popular culture on the other hand, refers to the cultural practices of large, heterogeneous societies that share many habits and characteristics. The elements of popular culture look similar in different places, and result in a relatively uniform landscape. Artifacts include music, food, entertainment, fashion, recreation, and various forms of art.

Folk culture diffuses slowly, on a small scale, usually through **relocation diffusion**. The Amish culture in the United States is a good example of the diffusion of a folk culture. Popular culture is easily diffused around the world, largely through **hierarchical diffusion**. The globalization of soccer is an example of the transformation and diffusion of an English folk culture to a popular culture.

Key Issues Revisited

4.1. Where Are Folk and Popular Leisure Activities Distributed?

- As a result of distinctive processes of origin and diffusion, folk and popular cultures have different distribution patterns

- Folk culture is more likely to have an anonymous origin and to diffuse slowly through migration

- Popular culture is more likely to be invented and diffused rapidly with the use of modern communications

Review Questions

4.1.1. All of the following are examples of folk music EXCEPT:

A. songs that deal with agriculture.

B. songs that deal with birth.

C. songs that deal with death.

D. songs that are made for the sole purpose of sales.

E. songs that deal with harvests.

4.1.2. Folk culture is primary spread through

A. TV.

B. radio stations.

C. the Internet.

D. social media.

E. relocation.

KEY ISSUE 2

Where Are Folk and Popular Material Culture Distributed?

Learning Outcome 4.2.1: Compare reasons for distribution of clothing styles in folk and popular culture.

Folk clothing is more likely to respond to environmental conditions and cultural values, whereas clothing styles vary more in time than in place.

Learning Outcome 4.2.2: Understand reasons for folk food preferences and taboos.

Folk food culture is especially strongly embedded in environmental conditions.

Learning Outcome 4.2.3: Describe regional variations in popular food preferences.

Popular food culture can display some regional variations.

Learning Outcome 4.2.4: Understand factors that influence patterns of folk housing.

Folk housing styles, like other folk material culture, respond to environmental and cultural factors.

Learning Outcome 4.2.5: Understand variations in time and space of housing in the United States.

U.S. housing has roots in folk culture, but newer housing displays features of popular culture.

Many different groups who are living in relative isolation practice folk cultures. They are especially susceptible to the various ways in which the physical environment can limit their activities and diffusion, because of their low level of technology. Thus their cultural identity and landscapes will be very diverse. For example there are many different types of Himalayan art in a relatively small geographic area because of the harsh physical environment and limited interaction. Housing provides another good example of the diversity of folk culture that results from the interaction of cultural and physical geography. The resultant landscapes exemplify distinctive and unique senses of place.

Cultural traits such as food, clothing, and housing are influenced by physical geography. Folk cultural traits, such as housing (**folk housing** or **indigenous architecture**) are especially responsive to the environment because of their low level of technology and utilization of available resources. The sum of the effects of the local environment on a specific food item is called **terroir**. It is commonly used to de-

---

scribe the way in which soil, climate, and other physical features influence the character of distinctive wines. Restrictions on certain behaviors, like the consumption of particular foods, can also be imposed by social customs. This is called a **taboo**.

Key Issues Revisited

4.2. Where are folk and popular material culture distributed?

- Unique folk cultures arise because of the lack of interaction among groups

- Folk culture is more likely to be influenced by the local environment

Review Questions

4.2.1. Which item of clothing has been banned in some European countries?

A. blue jeans

B. burqa

C. poncho

D. dashikini

E. beret

4.2.2. Where would you find a bostan?

A. London

B. Madrid

C. Sydney

D. Istanbul

E. Tokyo

KEY ISSUE 3

Why Is Access to Folk and Popular Culture Unequal?

Learning Outcome 4.3.1: Describe the origin, diffusion, and distribution of TV around the world.

TV diffused during the twentieth century from the United States to Europe and then to developing countries.

Learning Outcome 4.3.2: Compare the diffusion of the Internet and social media with the diffusion of TV.

Diffusion of the Internet and of social media has followed the pattern of TV, but at a much faster rate.

Learning Outcome 4.3.3: Understand external and internal threats to folk culture posed by electronic media.

Folk culture may be threatened by the dominance of popular culture in the media and by decreasing ability to control people's access to the media.

Popular culture diffuses rapidly where high levels of technology allow people to acquire material possessions. The increasingly global world allows for the rapid diffusion and acceptance of the material and nonmaterial elements of popular culture. For example, as a result of the diffusion of popular culture, there are less regional differences in housing, clothing, and food in more developed countries. Television has played a major role in the diffusion of popular culture, especially since World War II. International rates of TV ownership have climbed rapidly in LDCs in the early twenty-first century, but there are still international differences in TV ownership.

In the last decade other electronic media have become important transmitters of popular culture. Internet service has diffused at a rapid pace, from 40 million Internet users worldwide in 1995 to 2.4 billion in 2012. Since their beginnings, Facebook, Twitter, and YouTube have also diffused rapidly, and what once was a phenomenon in the United States continues to diffuse rapidly.

Key Issues Revisited

4.3. Why is access to folk and popular culture unequal?

- Popular culture diffuses rapidly across the world, aided by modern communications, especially television

- Differences in popular culture are more likely to be observed in one place at different points in time then among different places at one point in time

Review Questions

4.3.1. People in which country are most likely to watch the most TV?

A. South Korea

B. England

C. Russia

D. Uruguay

E. United States

4.3.2. According to the OpenNet Initiative, what content may governments block on the Internet?

A. political content

B. sexual content

C. security content

D. e-mail

E. all of the above

KEY ISSUE 4

Why Do Folk and Popular Culture Face Sustainability Challenges?

Learning Outcome 4.4.1: Summarize challenges for folk culture from diffusion of popular culture.

Popular culture threatens traditional elements of cultural identity in folk culture.

Learning Outcome 4.4.2: Summarize the two principal ways that popular culture can adversely affect the environment.

Popular culture can deplete scarce resources and pollute the landscape.

Learning Outcome 4.4.3: Summarize major sources of waste and the extent to which each is recycled.

Paper is the principal source of solid waste before recycling, but plastics and food waste are the leading sources after recycling.

The traditional role of women in developing counties is changing as a result of the diffusion of popular culture. It is leading to the advancement of women through education and economic and social opportunities. However it may also lead to negative impacts such as sex crimes against women.

The diffusion of popular culture threatens the survival of folk culture. It is one example of **cultural imperialism**, causing people to lose their traditional ways of life in favor of the material elements of popular culture from more developed countries. For example the Western dominance of the television industry, especially the news media, threatens the independence of less developed countries. Three MDCs —the United States, the United Kingdom, and Japan—dominate the television industry in LDCs. The diffusion of information to newspapers around the world is dominated by the Associated Press (AP) and Reuters, which are owned by U.S. and British companies, respectively. In recent years the diffusion of small satellite dishes, especially in countries where the government attempts to control the media, has influenced political change.

The creation of uniform landscapes through the diffusion of popular culture can negatively impact the environment by depleting natural resources and polluting the landscape. Golf courses remake the environment as do some types of commercial agriculture, and the demand for some products puts a strain on natural resources. Popular cultures such as fast-food generate more waste and thus lead to the pollution of the environment.

Key Issues Revisited

4.4. Why do folk and popular culture face sustainability challenges?

- Popular culture, usually originating in Western MDCs, may cause the elimination of some folk culture (globalization versus local diversity)

- Popular culture may adversely affect the environment

Review Questions

4.4.1. Amish folk culture originated in

A. Bern, Switzerland.

B. Berlin, Germany.

C. Brussels, Belgium.

D. Vienna, Austria.

E. Budapest, Hungary.

4.4.2. Which government has passed anti-dowry laws?

A. Afghanistan.

B. India.

C. United States.

D. Pakistan.

E. Bhutan.

Key Terms

Built environment

Cultural imperialism

Custom

Folk culture

Folk housing

Folklore

Folk songs

Habit

Hearths

Hierarchical diffusion

Indigenous architecture

Material culture

Popular culture

Relocation diffusion

Taboo

Terroir

Think Like a Geographer Activities

Research McDonald's fast food restaurant (http://www.aboutmcdonalds.com/country/map.html) in four different countries around the world. Explain the effects of popular culture on each, as well as clues that illustrate their local diversity.

Quick Quiz

4.1. A group's material culture is produced by

A. its geographic location.

B. its habits.

C. its food choices.

D. its food taboos.

E. a collection of social customs.

4.2. An example of an external threat to folk culture includes all but which of the following?

A. Facebook

B. MTV

C. CNN

D. Radio 1

E. The New York Times

4.3. In what ways does popular culture threaten environmental sustainability?

A. through recycling plans

B. because of increased demand for animal products

C. through curbside programs

D. because of decreased demand for golfing

E. because people are becoming vegans

4.4. Briefly describe how social media can affect a country's folk culture. Do you have any contemporary examples of where this has occurred?

Free Response

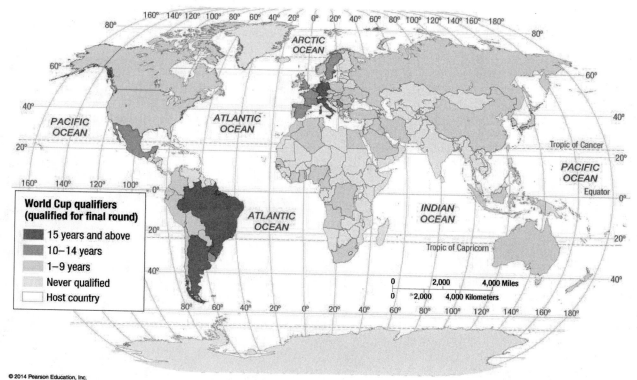

© 2014 Pearson Education, Inc.

Figure 4-1 Global Sports: World Cup

A. Look at the map above. Describe how a sport, such as soccer (football), can be transformed from a folk custom to part of the global popular culture.
B. What evidence from the map and your knowledge illustrates the global popularity of soccer?

On the Web

http://geography.about.com/od/culturalgeography/a/culturehearths.htm
http://www.loc.gov/folklife/archive.html
http://www.folkculturebh.org/en/
http://pcaaca.org/

Key Figures

Figure 4-12 Global Sports: World Cup
Figure 4-26 U.S. House Types 1945 to present
Figure 4-31 How Americans Spend Their Weekend
Figure 4-32 Diffusion of the Internet

Chapter

5 Languages

Where Are Languages Distributed?

This chapter discusses language which, together with religion and ethnicity, is one of the three traits that best distinguishes cultural values. The chapter looks at where languages are spoken and why they have distinctive distributions. As well as addressing the globalization of English, the chapter also examines attempts to preserve local languages. The global distribution of languages results from a combination of interaction and isolation.

Learning Outcome 5.1.1 Name the largest language families.

The two largest language families are Indo-European and Sino-Tibetan.

Learning Outcome 5.1.2: Identify the names and distribution of the two largest language families.

Indo-European is the predominant language family of Europe, Latin America, North America, South Asia, and South Pacific. Sino-Tibetan is the predominant language family of East Asia.

Learning Outcome 5.1.3: Identify the names and distribution of the largest language families in addition to Indo-European and Sino-Tibetan.

In addition to Indo-European and Sino-Tibetan, most of the world's remaining major language families are centered in Asia.

The English language became a distinct language in England as a result of westward Celtic migration, as well as the Germanic and Norman invasions. Modern English evolved mainly from the languages spoken by the German conquerors of Britain, the Angles, Saxons, and the Jutes (the word *England* comes from the *Angles 'land),* and changed again with the arrival of the Normans in 1066. Modern English emerged from a mingling of French and Germanic. English diffused around the world during Britain's era of colonialism.

Different dialects of a language develop through isolation from other speakers of the same language as well as by interaction with other speakers of that language. English has many dialects but **British Received Pronunciation (BRP),** the dialect associated with upper-class Britons, is recognized as the **standard language** which is the most accepted dialect for mass communication. In France the Parisian dialect became the standard form of French.

There are major dialect differences in English within Britain and the United States. Words that are associated with a dialect, such as the word that is used by children in Britain in a game of tag to signal that they have touched another participant, are spoken in a specific geographic region and thus have boundaries. This word-usage boundary is known as an **isogloss.**

Key Issues Revisited

5.1. Where are languages distributed?

- English can be traced to the invasions of England by Germanic tribes in the Dark Ages

- English diffused around the world from England as a result of colonialism

- Americans and English speak different dialects of English

Review Questions

5.1.1. The official language of China and Taiwan is

A. Han Chinese.

B. Tibetan Chinese.

C. Mandarin Chinese.

D. Manchurian Chinese.

E. English.

5.1.2. About 95% of the people in sub-Saharan Africa speak languages from which family?

A. Sino-Tibetan

B. Nilo-Saharan

C. Niger-Congo

D. Uralic

E. Indo-European

KEY ISSUE 2

Why Is English Related to Other Languages?

Learning Outcome 5.2.1: Learn the distribution of the Germanic and Indo-Iranian branches of Indo-European.

The four largest branches of Indo-European are Indo-Iranian, Romance, Germanic, and Balto-Slavic.

Learning Outcome 5.2.2: Learn the distribution of the Balto-Slavic and Romance branches of Indo-European.

Balto-Slavic predominates in Eastern Europe, Romance in Southern Europe and Latin America, Germanic in Northern Europe and North America, and Indo-Iranian in South Asia and Central Asia.

Learning Outcome 5.2.3: Understand the origin and diffusion of English.

English is a Germanic branch language because German-speaking tribes invaded England more than 1,500 years ago. Romance branch words entered English after French-speaking Normans invaded England nearly 1,000 years ago.

Learning Outcome 5.2.4: Understand the two theories of the origin and diffusion of Indo-European.

Indo-European originated before recorded history; two competing theories disagree on whether origin and diffusion occurred primarily because of conquest (war) or peace (agriculture). The diffusion of Romance languages 2,000 years ago is well documented through the spread of the Roman Empire.

Language is one of the oldest and most geographically diverse cultural traits on Earth. It is a system of communication through speech. Many languages have a **literary tradition,** although some have only an **oral tradition.**

All languages belong to a **language family** which is a collection of many languages that were originally related through a common ancestor. The **Indo-European family** is the world's most spoken language family. A **language branch** is a collection of languages related through a common ancestor within a language family, although not as old. Germanic is one of the branches of the Indo-European language family. A **language group** is a set of languages within a branch that share a relatively recent common origin. English is a language in the West Germanic group of the Germanic group of the Indo-European family. **Dialects** are regionally distinct versions of a single language that are distinguished by vocabulary, spelling, and pronunciation. **Ebonics** is an African-American dialect in the United States. British and American English are examples of different dialects of English. Countries designate at least one language as their **official language,** which is used for all government business. A **monolingual state** will only have one official language that is used in this capacity. **Multilingual states,** such as Kenya (Swahili and English) and Switzerland (German, French, Italian and Romansh), have more than one official language. Belgium is a multilingual state because French and Flemish (a dialect of the Germanic language of Dutch) are both official languages, but the country has had more difficulty reconciling the interests of the different language speakers. **English** is known as a **lingua franca** because it is a language of international communication.

Languages of the Indo-European family are spoken on all continents but are dominant in Europe and the Americas. There are eight branches of the Indo-European family. Large numbers of people speak a language of one of the following four branches: Indo-Iranian, Romance, Germanic, and Balto-Slavic.

German and English are both part of the Germanic branch of Indo-European. The branch of Indo-European with the most speakers is Indo-Iranian, which is divided into an eastern group (Indie), and a western group (Iranian). Hindi is the most spoken of the eastern group and Pakistan's principal language, Urdu, is essentially the same but written in the Arabic alphabet. The major Iranian group languages include Persian, Pashto, and Kurdish.

The Balto-Slavic languages are largely those of Eastern Europe, especially Russian. The Romance languages, including Spanish, Portuguese, French, Italian, and Romanian, all developed from the Latin language of the Romans. Provincial people in the Roman Empire spoke a common form of Latin known as **Vulgar Latin.** Latin diffused with the expansion of the Roman republic and empire, and much later, during the era of Spanish and Portuguese imperialism in the Americas.

There are two theories about the origin and diffusion of Indo-European. The **Nomadic Warrior Thesis** or theory of Kurgan origin states that the first Indo-European speakers were Kurgans who lived near present-day Russia and Kazakhstan. They migrated westward into Europe, southward to Iran and South Asia, and eastward into Siberia, largely by military conquest. The theory of Anatolian origin states that the first speakers of Proto-Indo-European lived in eastern Anatolia two thousand years before the Kurgans, and that they migrated west into Europe and east into Asia with their agricultural practices, rather than by military conquest. Regardless of how Indo-European diffused, communication was poor and the result was isolation. Ultimately distinct languages evolved from distinct groups.

Key Issues Revisited

5.2. Why is English related to other languages?

- English is part of the Germanic branch of the Indo-European language family

- Nearly one-half of the worlds speak a language in the Indo-European family

- Indo-European languages developed from a single ancestor through migration, followed by isolation of one group from others

Review Questions

5.2.1. Which language is derived from Old Norse?

A. Swedish

B. Danish

C. Norwegian

D. Icelandic

E. All of these

5.2.2. Devanagari is the script in which what language is written?

A. Tamil

B. Sindhi

C. Hindi

D. Oryia

E. Marathi

KEY ISSUE 3

Why Do Individual Languages Vary among Places?

Learning Outcome 5.3.1: Describe the main dialects in the United States

U.S. English is divided into four main dialects. Differences can be traced to patterns of migration to the American colonies from various parts of England.

Learning Outcome 5.3.2: Understand the main ways that British and U.S. dialects vary.

British and American dialects vary by vocabulary, spelling, and pronunciation.

Learning Outcome 5.3.3: Understand why it is sometimes difficult to distinguish between a language and a dialect.

The distinction is often based on political decisions rather than the actual characteristics of the languages or dialects.

The second largest language family is **Sino-Tibetan,** spoken by nearly twenty percent of the world's population. It includes most of Southeast Asia and China, which is the world's most populous state. The languages of China, of which Mandarin is the most important and widely spoken, generally belong to the Sinitic branch of the Sino-Tibetan family. Unlike Indo-European languages, Chinese languages are based on one-syllable words and have thousands of characters. Most of these characters are **logograms,** which represent ideas or concepts rather than specific pronunciations. Other East and Southeast Asian language families include Japanese, Korean, Austro-Asiatic, and Austronesian. TaiKadai, once classified as a branch of the Sino-Tibetan family, is also an Asian language family, spoken in Thailand

and neighboring portions of China. The major language families of the Middle East and Central Asia include Afro-Asiatic, Altaic, and Uralic (which was once classified with Altaic). More than 95% of the people in sub-Saharan Africa speak languages of the Niger-Congo, especially Swahili. Other African language families include Nilo-Saharan and Khoisan.

Key Issues Revisited

5.3. Why do individual languages vary among places?

- Nearly one-fourth of the world speaks a language in the Sino-Tibetan family

- A half-dozen other language families encompass another one-fourth of the world

- Each language has a distinctive distribution, which is a result of a combination of migration and isolation

Review Questions

5.3.1. An isogloss is used by geographers to

A. determine climate zones.

B. determine global warming.

C. determine word choices.

D. identify polar melting rates.

E. identify isolated groups.

5.3.2. Why is the English spoken in American so different than that spoken in Britain?

A. The colonists rebelled and refused to speak the same way.

B. People in America did not know how to spell so changes happened.

C. The Native Indians changed the words.

D. Isolation from Britain created the change.

E. George Washington passed an executive order to create the changes.

KEY ISSUE 4

Why Do People Preserve Local Languages?

Learning Outcome 5.4.1: Understand how several countries peacefully embrace more than one language.
Switzerald, Belgium, and Nigeria have varying approaches to multilingual societies.

Learning Outcome 5.4.2: Understand what is meant by an isolated language and an extinct language.

Thousands of languages once in use are now extinct. Some isolated languages survive that are unrelated to any other.

Learning Outcome 5.4.3: Understand why the number of Celtic speakers has declined and how the languages are being pr served.

Celtic languages were widely spoken in the British Isles before the Germanic invasions. These languages are being preserved through the efforts of advocacy groups and government agencies.

Learning Outcome 5.4.4: Understand the concept of a lingua franca.

A lingua franca is a language of international communication. English is currently the world's most widely used lingua franca.

Learning Outcome 5.4.5: Understand how English has diffused to other languages.

English is being combined with other languages, such as French and Spanish.

Learning Outcome 5.4.6: Understand the role of Spanish and French in North America.

French is widely used in Canada, especially in Québec. Spanish is widely used in the United States, especially in the Southwest.

Thousands of languages are **extinct languages,** once in existence but no longer in use today. The European language of Gothic is such an example. Languages can become extinct through the loss of an entire people or through linguistic evolution over time. However the pressures of economic and social **acculturation,** the **assimilation** of cultural traits such as language by one group under the influence of another, are responsible for most of today's losses. Many African languages have become extinct because of the linguistic effects of European colonialism. Globalization today threatens many languages in the world.

Hebrew is a rare example of an extinct language that has been revived. The revival of this language is associated with the Zionist movement and the creation of the state of Israel in 1948. 1t is one symbol of Israeli nationalism.

Endangered languages, such as those belonging to the Celtic branch of Indo-European, are experiencing resurgence today. The revival of Irish Gaelic, Scottish Gaelic, and Brythonic (Welsh) is linked to nationalistic movements in these parts of the British Isles. Other Celtic languages include Cornish and Breton.

When two groups of people with different languages meet, a new language with some characteristics of each may result so that they can communicate. This is called a **pidgin language**. Where the linguistic traditions of indigenous peoples and colonizers have blended, a **Creole language** will result. This has occurred in Louisiana and is one symbol of the distinctive culture that has developed in this region of the United States.

Languages develop and change as a result of diffusion and interaction among people. The widespread use of English in the French language is called **Franglais**, and the diffusion of English into the Spanish language is called **Spanglish**. **Denglish** is a combination of German and English. However some languages lack interaction with speakers of other languages. An **isolated language,** such as Basque in the Pyrenees Mountains, is one that is unrelated to any other language family.

Key Issues Revisited

5.4. Why do people preserve local languages?

- English has become the most important language for international communication

- As a result of the global dominance of a lingua franca such as English, less widely used languages can become endangered or extinct

- Some local languages are being preserved and revived because they are an important element of cultural identity

Review Questions

5.4.1. An example of a multilingual state would be

A. Belgium.

B. Costa Rica.

C. Portugal.

D. Mexico.

E. Ireland.

5.4.2. An example of an isolated language is

A. English.

B. Hebrew.

C. Gaelic.

D. Basque.

E. Gothic.

Key Terms

Acculturation	Language group
Assimilation	Lingua franca
British Received Pronunciation (BRP)	Literary tradition
Creole or creolized language	Logograms
Denglish	Monolingual country
Dialect	Multilingual country
Ebonics	Nomadic Warrior Thesis
Extinct Language	Official language
Franglais	Oral tradition
Indo-European family	Pidgin language
Isogloss	Sino-Tibetan family
Isolated language	Spanglish
Language	Standard language
Language branch	Vulgar Latin
Language family	

Think Like a Geographer Activities

http://http://www.ethnologue.com
Go to the link above and explore languages that are extinct or on the verge of going extinct. Can you explain the impact of language extinction in terms of a country's culture, literary traditions, and local diversity?

Describe how the diffusion of a lingua franca has changed over time.

Quick Quiz:

5.1. Which language family does English belong to?
A. Sino-Tibetan
B. Sino-European
C. Indo-European
D. Indo-Caucasian
E. Niger-Congo

5.2. Which language family does Mandarin belong to?
A. Sino-Tibetan
B. Sino-European
C. Indo-European
D. Indo-Caucasian
E. Niger-Congo

5.3. Why does the Korean language differ from Sino-Tibetan languages?
A. It is written with logograms.
B. It is written with ideograms.
C. It is written in hangul.
D. It is written in Cyrillic.
E. It is written in the Roman alphabet.

5.4. After 1066 the official language in England was
A. German.
B. Celtic.
C. Gaelic.
D. French.
E. English.

5.5. Which country has four official languages?
A. Spain
B. Canada
C. Switzerland
D. Nigeria
E. Japan

Free Response

**Figure 5.2—Penmachno, Wales
(photo courtesy of Tony Hurt)**

**Figure 5.1—Penmachno, Wales
(photo courtesy of Tony Hurt)**

With reference to the photos above, identify and explain at least three reasons why the government of Wales would have bilingual signs throughout their country.

On the Web

http://www.masteringgeography.com
http://www.infoplease.com/ipa/A0855611.html
https://www.cia.gov/library/publications/the-world-factbook/fields/2098.html
http://geography.about.com/od/culturalgeography/a/linguafranca.htm
http://www.culturalsurvival.org/programs/elc/program

Key Figures

Figure 5-3 Language Family Tree
Figure 5-5 Distribution of Language Families
Figure 5-8 Africa's Language Families
Figure 5-42 English- Speaking Countries

Chapter

6 Religions

Where Are Religions Distributed?

The distribution and diffusion of major religions is outlined. The chapter also explains why certain religions have not diffused widely. The chapter goes on to discuss the relationship between religions and the physical environment. Finally religious conflict is addressed.

Learning Outcome 6.1.1: Describe the distribution of the major religions.

Christianity predominates in Europe and the Western Hemisphere, Buddhism in East Asia, Hinduism in South Asia, and Islam in other regions of Asia, as well as North Africa.

Learning Outcome 6.1.2: Describe the distribution of the major branches of Christianity.

Christianity is divided into three main branches: Roman Catholic, which predominates in southwest Europe and Latin America; Protestant, which predominates in northwest Europe and North America; and Orthodox, which predominates in Eastern Europe.

Learning Outcome 6.1.3: Identify the major branches of Islam and Buddhism.

Islam's two major branches are Sunni and Shiite. The two largest branches of Buddhism are Mahayana and Theravada.

Learning Outcome 6.1.4: Describe the distribution of the largest ethnic religions.

Hinduism is clustered primarily in India. Other ethnic religions with the largest numbers of followers are clustered elsewhere in Asia.

As a cultural trait, **religion** helps to define people and how they understand the world around them. There are essentially two major types of religions, universalizing and ethnic. **Universalizing religions** appeal to people of many cultures, regardless of where they live in the world. Nearly 58% of the world's population adheres to a universalizing religion. **Ethnic religions** appeal primarily to one group of people living in one place. About 26% of the world's population follows an ethnic religion. Some religions are **monotheistic,** teaching the primacy of one god, whereas other religions are **polytheistic,** teaching that there are numerous gods. **Atheists** do not believe in any god.

Buddhism, Christianity, and Islam are the three major universalizing or **global religions.** Each is divided into branches, denominations, and sects. A **branch** is a fundamental division within a religion. A **denomination** is a division of a branch; this term is most commonly used to describe the Protestant denominations of Christianity. A **sect** is a group that is smaller than a denomination.

Buddhism is the oldest of the world's universalizing religions, with millions of adherents clustered in East and Southeast Asia. Founded by Siddhartha Gautama in the sixth century B.C., Buddhism teaches that suffering originates from our attachment to life and other worldly possessions. The key concepts of Buddhism are outlined in the Four Noble Truths. Buddhism split into three main branches, Vajrayana, Theravada and Mahayana, as followers disagreed on interpreting statements by Siddhartha Gautama. Theravada Buddhism is found mainly in Cambodia, Laos, Myanmar, Sri Lanka, and Thailand. Mahayana Buddhism is more prevalent in China, Japan, and Korea. The Vajrayanist are found mainly in Mongolia and Tibet. Unlike Christians and Muslims, most Buddhists also follow an ethnic religion too.

Christianity has about two billion adherents and is the world's most geographically widespread religion. Christians believe in one God and that his son, Jesus, was the promised Messiah, delivering salvation to all people. Christianity has three major branches: Roman Catholic, Eastern Orthodox, and Protestant. The Roman Catholic Church, with its hearth at Vatican City in Rome, is the most important religion in large parts of Europe and North America, and is dominant in Latin America. Catholicism also exists on other continents. The Protestant Church began in the 1500s with Martin Luther's protests against the abuses of the Catholic Church. It is the most important religion in large parts of northern Europe as well as the regions of North America to which many people from northern Europe migrated. As with the Catholic Church, Protestantism also has adherents on other continents.

The Eastern Orthodox branch of Christianity is only dominant in Eastern Europe and Russia, but also has adherents in smaller populations throughout the world.

Islam, with more than 1.5 billion followers, is the dominant religion in North Africa and the Middle East, as well as Bangladesh and Indonesia. The Muslin population in North America and Europe has increased dramatically in recent years. Islam is a monotheistic religion, based on the belief that there is one God, Allah, and that Mohammed was Allah's prophet. The word *Islam* in Arabic means *submission to the will of God,* and an adherent is a Muslim or *one who surrenders to God.* Islam is divided into two branches: *Sunni,* which is by far the larger of the two, and *Shiite.* In recent years there has been a rise in radical **fundamentalism** that has caused more division and conflict in the Muslim world. Most fundamentalists accept the holy book of Islam, the Koran, as the unquestioned guide on both religious and secular matters. Islamic fundamentalism avoids any sort of Western influence and can contribute to intense conflict.

Sikhism and **Baha'i** are the two universalizing religions other than Buddhism, Christianity, and Islam with the largest number of followers. Most Sikhs are located in the Punjab region of India, whereas Baha'is are dispersed among many countries, especially in Africa and Asia.   **Hinduism,** with nearly 900 million adherents, is the largest ethnic religion and the world's third largest religion. Ethnic religions have much more clustered distributions than universalizing religions; the vast majority of Hindus live on the Indian subcontinent. For thousands of years Hindus in India have developed a unique society that integrates spiritual practices with daily life. Hindus believe that there is more than one path to reach God; there are thousands of deities in the Hindu belief system and thus the religion is polytheistic.

The other major ethnic religion is **Judaism**, which was the first major monotheistic religion. Both Christianity and Judaism have some of their roots in Judaism; Jesus was born a Jew, and Mohammed traced his ancestry to Abraham. Judaism is based on a sense of ethnic identity in the lands bordering the eastern Mediterranean. Jewish people have been returning to this land since the end of the nineteenth century, and in 1948 the Jewish state of Israel was created. Today most Jews live in Israel and the United States.

Other ethnic religions particularly found in China are **syncretic**, meaning they are a combination of several different religions or traditional practices; **Confucianism** and **Taoism** (sometimes spelled Daoism) are sometimes distinguished as philosophies more than ethnic religions. There is a lot of mixing of these philosophies and religions. Some Africans still practice **animism**, or traditional ethnic religions, although there has been a rapid decline in African animism because of the increase in the numbers of Christians and Muslims.

Key Issues Revisited

6.1. Where are religions distributed?

- The world has three large universalizing religions—Christianity, Islam, and Buddhism—each with their own distinctive distribution

- Hinduism is the largest ethnic religion, and most of its adherents are clustered in India

Review Questions

6.1.1. The largest ethnic religion by far is

A. Jutche.

B. Baha'ism.

C. Shintoism.

D. Hinduism.

E. Islam.

6.1.2 All of these are part of the Christian church EXCEPT

A. Daoism.

B. Roman Catholic.

C. Protestant.

D. Eastern Orthodox.

E. Russian Orthodox.

KEY ISSUE 2

Why Do Religions Have Different Distributions?

Learning Outcome 6.2.1: Describe the process of origin of universalizing religions.

A universalizing religion originated with a single historical individual.

Learning Outcome 6.2.2: Understand differences in the origin of universalizing and ethnic religions.

Ethnic religions typically have unknown origins.

Learning Outcome 6.2.3: Describe the process of diffusion of universalizing religions.

Universalizing religions have diffused from their place of origin to other regions of the world.

Learning Outcome 6.2.4: Compare the diffusion of universalizing and ethnic religions.

Ethnic religions typically do not diffuse far from their place of origin.

The three universalizing religions diffused from **hearths,** or places of origin that are associated with the lives of their founders. Christianity diffused through relocation diffusion where **missionaries** carried the teachings of Jesus around the Mediterranean world. Expansion diffusion was also important as **pagans,** followers of ancient polytheistic religions, were converted to Christianity. It diffused beyond the European realm during the age of colonialism beginning in the early 1500s.

Islam diffused from its hearth at Mecca through military conquest across North Africa, Southern Europe, and other parts of Southwest Asia. Arab traders brought the religion to sub-Saharan Africa and later Indonesia.

Buddhism diffused from its hearth in northern India to the island of Ceylon (present day Sri Lanka) and eastwards into East and Southeast Asia as a result of missionary activity and trade.

Universalizing religions have supplanted and mingled with ethnic religions in various parts of the world. In some parts of Africa that were colonized by Europeans, Christianity has replaced animistic religions.

In other parts of the continent the two have merged. In East Asia, especially Japan, Buddhism and Shintoism have merged.

Since Roman times Jews have been forced to leave the eastern Mediterranean and disperse throughout the world, an action known as the **diaspora** (from the Greek word for *dispersion)*. Historically Jews were persecuted and forced to live in **ghettos**, city areas set up by law to be inhabited only by Jews, in many European countries. Since the Nazi Holocaust many Jews have returned to the Middle East and today Israel is a Jewish state, although Judaism, unlike other ethnic religions, is practiced in many countries.

Key Issues Revisited

6. 2. Why do religions have different distributions?

- Universalizing religions have a known origin and clear pattern of diffusion

- Ethnic religions usually have unknown origins and little diffusion

- Holy places and holidays in a universalizing religion are related to events in the life of its founder or prophet

- Holy places and holidays in an ethnic religion are related to the local physical geography

Review Questions

6.2.1   What form of Buddhism believes that people must give up worldly possessions and become a monk?

A. Zen

B. Hinayana

C. Theravada

D. Mahayana

E. Chinese

6.2.2 Muhammad's migration from Makkah to Yathrib is known as

A. the salat.

B. the hajj.

C. the zakat.

D. the hijra.

E. the trek.

KEY ISSUE 3

Why Do Religions Organize Space in Distinctive Patterns?

Learning Outcome 6.3.1: Compare the role of places of worship in various religions.

Religions have places of worship, but these places play differing roles for the various religions.

Learning Outcome 6.3.2: Explain why places are sacred in universalizing religions.

In universalizing religions, holy places derive from events in the founder's life.

Learning Outcome 6.3.3: Analyze the importance of the physical geography in ethnic religions.

In ethnic religions, holy places derive from the physical geography where the religion's adherents are clustered.

Learning Outcome 6.3.4: Describe ways in which the landscape is used in religiously significant ways.

Religions have varying practices for handling the dead.

Learning Outcome 6.3.5: Compare the calendars and holidays of ethnic and universalizing religions.

In ethnic religions, holidays derive from the physical geography where the religion is clustered.

Learning Outcome 6.3.6: Compare the administrative organization of hierarchical and locally autonomous religions.

Religions can be divided into those that are administered through a hierarchy and those that are locally autonomous.

Both universalizing and ethnic religions have holy places that are usually associated with the history of that religion. Adherents will make a religions journey or **pilgrimage** to holy places.

Buddhist holy places or shrines mark the location of important events in Buddha's life and are in northern India and southern Nepal. Lumbini in southern Nepal is where Buddha was born and is considered the holiest site for Buddhist. The holiest locations in Islam are associated with the life of Mohammed, and include, in order of importance, Makkah (Mecca), Madinah (Medina), and Jerusalem. Holy places in ethnic religions are closely tied to physical geography. For example, to Hindus the River Ganges is the holiest river in India and they believe that bathing in its waters will achieve purification.

Universalizing and ethnic religions have a different understanding of the relationship between people and their environment. This is exemplified in their different attitudes towards **cosmogony**, the set of religious beliefs that concern the origin of the universe, and the calendar, which for ethnic religions is very much tied to physical geography. The **solstice** has special significance in some ethnic religions and has its origins in some pagan religions.

The Roman Catholic Church is a good example of a **hierarchical religion**, with its well-defined geographical structure and division of territory into local administrative units. Archbishops report to the pope and each heads a **province.** Bishops report to archbishops and administer a **diocese**, which is the basic unit of the geographic organization of the Roman Catholic Church. The headquarters of a bishop is called a *see* and is usually the largest city in the diocese. A priest reports to a bishop and heads a **parish**.

Islam and some Protestant denominations are good examples of **autonomous religions** because they are relatively self-sufficient with little interaction between communities within the religion.

Religion impacts the landscape in a variety of ways. Christian churches were originally modeled after Roman basilicas. Mosques are the most important religious buildings in the Islamic world, and they also serve as places for the community to gather. Most Hindus worship at home although Hindu temples serve as shrines to one or more of their gods. The pagoda is the most visible religious architecture of the Buddhist and Shintoist landscape, and contains the relics of Buddhism.

Burial practices of different religions are also visible on the landscape. Christians, Muslims, and Jews usually bury their dead in cemeteries.

Place names or toponyms also show the impact of religion on the landscape. For example many Roman Catholic places are named for saints. Religious buildings, places of pilgrimage, burial locations, and place names are all examples of **sacred spaces**.

Cremation has replaced burial as a means of disposing of the dead in many parts of the world because of the pressure on agricultural land. This is particularly true in China and Western Europe. Cremation is also used in the Hindu world although it is putting an increasing strain on India's wood supplies.

The calendar is also an important part of life in both universalizing and ethnic religions. Judaism is considered an ethnic rather than a universalizing religion partly because its events are held in conjunction with the agricultural calendar. Universalizing religions' calendars are based on events dealing with the founder's life.

Key Issues Revisited

6.3. Why do religions organize space in distinctive patterns?

- Some religions have elaborate places of worship

- Religions affect the landscape in other ways too, including the building of religious communities, toponyms marking the landscape, and land reserved for burying the dead

- Some universalizing religions organize their territory into a rigid administrative structure

Review Questions

6.3.1. Which is not a sanctified place?

A. Salisbury Cathedral

B. Notre Dame Cathedral

C. Salt Lake Temple

D. The Blue Mosque

E. The Washington Cathedral

6.3.2. The holiest river for Hindus is

A. The Po.

B. The Lena.

C. The Ganges.

D. The Indus.

E. The Brahmaputra.

KEY ISSUE 4

Why Do Territorial Conflicts Arise Among Religious Groups?

Learning Outcome 6.4.1: Understand reasons for religious conflicts arising from government policies.

Religions can come into conflict with government policies, social changes, or other religions.

Learning Outcome 6.4.2: Summarize reasons for conflicts between religions.

Conflicts among religions have been especially strong in Ireland and in the Middle East.

Learning Outcome 6.4.3: Analyze reasons for religious conflict in the Middle East.

Religious conflict in the Middle East goes back thousands of years. Jews, Muslims, and Christians have fought for control of the Middle East land that is now part of Israel/Palestine.

Learning Outcome 6.4.4: Describe differences in geographic frameworks in the Middle East.

Combatants in the Middle East have different perspectives on the division of land in the area.

Learning Outcome 6.4.5: Explain the importance of Jerusalem to Jews and Muslims.

The most sacred space in Jerusalem for Muslims was built on top of the most sacred space for Jews.

Religious identification can lead to religious conflict. When looking at religious conflict, geographers tend to look at these conflicts as conflicts caused by one of the following: religion versus government policies, religion versus social change, religion versus religion, or religious wars in the Middle East. The Hindu **caste system**, which was the hereditary class into which a Hindu was placed according to religious law, has led to social and ethnic conflict in India. These issues are less significant now that the caste system has been legally abolished. The rise of communism has also been a challenge to organized religion, especially in Eastern Europe and Asia.

Religious conflict continues in many parts of the world especially at the boundaries between different religions, branches, and denominations. These conflicts have complex historical, social, and ethnic roots and must be also understood in the context of political geography. For example there has been long-standing conflict in the Middle East. The city of Jerusalem contains sites that are sacred to Judaism, Christianity, and Islam. There have been religious wars in Ireland between Catholics and Protestants that have their origins in the English conquest of Ireland centuries ago. Tibetan Buddhism has been undermined by Chinese Communism since the latter's takeover of Tibet in 1950. There is concern that many Tibetan Buddhist traditions will be lost forever when the Dalai Lama and present generation of priests die.

Key Issues Revisited

6.4. Why do territorial conflicts arise among religions groups?

- Expansion of the territory occupied by one religion may reduce the territory of another

- Religions must compete for control of territory with nonreligious ideas, such as economic modernization

Review Questions

6.4.1. Which religion supports the caste system?

A. Buddhism

B. Catholicism

C. Islam

D. Hinduism

E. Baha'ism

6.4.2 Who described religion as the "opium of the people?"

A. Lenin

B. Stalin

C. Czar Nicholas

D. Marx

E. Engels

Key Terms

Animism	**Hierarchical religion**
Atheism	**Hinduism**
Autonomous religions	**Islam**
Baha'i	**Judaism**
Branch	**Missionary**
Buddhism	**Monotheism**
Caste system	**Pagan**
Christianity	**Parish**
Confucianism	**Pilgrimage**
Cosmogony	**Polygamy**
Taoism	**Polytheism**
Denomination	**Province**
Diaspora	**Religion**
Diocese	**Sacred Spaces**
Ethnic religion	**Sect**
Fundamentalism	**Shintoism**
Ghetto	**Sikhism**
Global religions	**Solstice**
Hearth	**Syncretic**
	Universalizing religion

Think Like a Geographer Activities

Research the recent conflict between Buddhists in Tibet and the communist government of China, as well as the conflict in Northern Ireland between the Catholics and the Protestants. Explain the impact of religion on the cultural landscape.

Quick Quiz

Who am I?

6.1. Born in Lumbini, Nepal
6.2. Bishop of the Diocese of Rome
6.3. Born in Makkah
6.4. I was exiled to Baghdad in 1853
6.5. Traveled in South Asia 500 years ago
to convert people to follow me

A. Guru Nanak
B. Buddha
C. Baha'u'llah
D. The Pope
E. Muhammad

Free Response Question

Figure 6.1

A. Identify the religious conflict that is illustrated in the photo.
B. Identify and explain three ways that religion causes conflicts.

On the Web

http://www.masteringgeography.com
http://www.religioustolerance.org/var_rel.htm
http://www.religionfacts.com/
http://www.infoplease.com/ipa/A0855613.html
http://www.adherents.com/

Key Figures

Figure 6-3 World Distributions of Religions
Figure 6-7 Distribution of Christians in the United States
Figure 6-8 Distribution of Muslims
Figure 6-18 Diffusion of Universalizing Religions
Figure 6-47 Distribution of Catholics and Protestants in Ireland
Figure 6-49 Boundary Changes in Israel/Palestine

Chapter

7 Ethnicities

Where Are Ethnicities Distributed?

The geographic distribution of ethnicities is initially considered in this chapter. Ethnic groups are tied to particular places because members of the group, or their ancestors, were born or raised there. Another important consideration here is ethnic conflict in specific areas of the world. The attempt to retain distinct ethnic identity is one example of the preservation of local diversity.

Learning Outcome 7.1.1: Identify and describe the major ethnicities in the United States.

The three most numerous ethnicities are Hispanics, African Americans, and Asian Americans.

Learning Outcome 7.1.2: Describe the distribution of major U.S. ethnicities among states and within urban areas.

Hispanics are clustered in the Southwest, African Americans in the Southeast, and Asian Americans in the West. African Americans and Hispanics are highly clustered in urban areas, especially in inner-city neighborhoods.

Ethnicity comes from the Greek root *ethnos, which* means *national.* Ethnicity is identity with a group of people who share a common identity with a specific homeland or hearth. It is distinct from **race**, which is identity with a group of people who share a biological ancestor. Biological classification by race is the basis for **racism**, which is the belief that racial differences produce an inherent superiority of a particular race. A **racist** is someone who follows the beliefs of racism. The characteristics of ethnicity derive from the distinctive features of specific geographic locations whereas those of race are not rooted in particular places.

The two most numerous ethnicities in the United States are Hispanics (or Latinos), at 15% of total population, and African Americans at 13%. About 4% are Asian-America and 1% American Indian. At a regional scale African-Americans are clustered in the Southeast, Hispanics in the Southwest, Asian-Americans in the West, and American Indians in the Southwest and Plains states. At the urban level African Americans and Hispanics are highly clustered in **ethnic neighborhoods,** especially in northern cities. At the same time these cities are also **multicultural**.

Discrimination by race was the cornerstone of the South African legal system of apartheid. **Apartheid** was the physical separation of different races into separate geographic areas. It was instituted by the white racist Afrikaners government in 1948, and was particularly designed to subjugate the black majority by forcing them to live in impoverished homelands. The apartheid laws were repealed in the 1990s, but although South Africa now has black majority rule, it will take many years to redress their geographic impact.

Three major migration patterns have shaped the present distribution of African Americans within the United States. The first was the forced migration from Africa that was part of the **triangular slave trade**. After slavery most African Americans remained in the rural South working as **sharecroppers**, farming land rented from a landowner and paying rent in the form of crops. Blacks were still separated from whites in the South through laws that followed the Supreme Court's "separate but equal" treatment of the races. The second major migration pattern was the migration to northern cities from the beginning of the twentieth century. In these cities, African American immigrants lived in **ghettos,** named for the term for neighborhoods where Jews were forced to live in medieval Europe. Segregation laws were eliminated during the 1950s and 1960s. The third migration pattern was their movement from ghettos into neighborhoods immediately adjacent during this time. This was made possible by "white flight" to the suburbs, which in turn was encouraged by **blockbusting**, where real estate agents convinced white homeowners living near a black area to sell their houses at low prices.

Key Issues Revisited

7.1. Where are ethnicities distributed?

- Major ethnicities in the United States include African Americans, Hispanic Americans, and Asian Americans

- These ethnic groups are clustered in regions of the country and within urban areas

- Sometimes race and ethnicity are used interchangeably

Review Questions

7.1.1. The most important feature of race that geographers look at is

A. skin color.

B. hair type.

C. hair color.

D. blood type.

E. facial features.

7.1.2. At what scale would the distribution of African Americans and Hispanics be most notable because they are so clustered together?

A. local scale

B. regional scale

C. county scale

D. state scale

E. national scale

KEY ISSUE 2

Why Do Ethnicities Have Distinctive Distributions?

Learning Outcome 7.2.1: Describe the patterns of forced and voluntary migration of African Americans, Hispanic Americans, and Asian Americans to the United States.

Many African Americans trace their ancestry to forced migration from Africa for slavery.

Many Hispanics and Asian Americans trace their heritage to people who migrated in the late twentieth century for economic prospects and political freedom.

Learning Outcome 7.2.2: Describe the patterns of migration of African Americans within the United States.

African Americans migrated in large numbers from the South to the North and West in the early twentieth century. African Americans clustered in inner-city ghettos that have expanded in recent decades.

Learning Outcome 7.2.3: Explain the laws once used to segregate races in the United States and South Africa.

Segregation of races was legal in the United States and South Africa until the late twentieth century.

Nationality, which comes from the Latin word *nasci,* meaning *to have been born,* is identity with a group of people who share legal attachment and personal allegiance to a country. The desire for self-rule or **self-determination** has transformed ethnic groups into nationalities. A **nation-state** is a state whose territory corresponds to that occupied by a particular ethnicity. There are numerous nation-states in Europe including France, Slovenia, and Denmark. However no nation-state consists entirely of people from the same ethnic group. For example there are some German speakers in Denmark, and some Danish speakers in Germany.

Nationalism refers to the degree of loyalty that one has for a nationality. This could be instilled by promoting symbols of nationalism such as flags and songs. Nationalism is an example of a **centripetal force**, which is one that tends to unify people behind the state. **Centrifugal forces** do exactly the opposite and may lead to the breakup of a state.

Multiethnic states contain more than one dominant ethnicity. For example Belgium is divided among the Dutch-speaking Flemish and the French-speaking Walloons. They are also called **multinational states,** and each ethnic group will generally recognize each other as distinct nationalities. This is true of the United Kingdom today with its four major nationalities—English, Welsh, Scottish, and (northern) Irish. All four field their own national soccer teams. The former Soviet Union was the largest multinational state with 15 republics that represented many different ethnic groups. Now they are independent states in the Baltic, Eastern Europe, Central Asia, and the Caucasus. There are geopolitical problems in the Caucasus because the boundaries of Armenia, Azerbaijan, and Georgia do not completely match the territories occupied by these ethnicities. For example there are minorities of Armenians in Azerbaijan and vice versa. Russia is still the largest multinational state with 39 nationalities, many of which, like Chechnya, want to be independent.

There has been a resurgence of ethnic identity and nationalism in Eastern Europe since the 1980s. Prior to the 1980s this was effectively suppressed by communist control. This has led to the breakup of the Soviet Union, Yugoslavia, and Czechoslovakia, and the emergence of smaller nation-states. Slovenia is a good example of a nation-state that emerged from the former Yugoslavia in the 1990s. Slovenes comprise more than 90% of the population of Slovenia; thus the country is relatively peaceful and stable. These movements for **self-determination** are fueled by **ethnonationalism**, a strong feeling of belonging to a nation that is a minority within a state.

Key Issues Revisited

7.2. Why do ethnicities have distinctive distributions?

- Nationalities are ethnic groups that are attached and loyal to a particular country

- Nationality combines an ethnic group's language, religion, history, and other patriotic events

- Many countries have been created in an attempt to transform single ethnic groups into single nationalities

Review Questions

7.2.1. What amendment to the constitution outlawed slavery?

A. Amendment 19

B. Amendment 14

C. Amendment 5

D. Amendment 13

E. Amendment 1

7.2.2. Which group encouraged "white flight?"

A. the federal government

B. the state government

C. real estate agents

D. scientists

E. physicians

KEY ISSUE 3

Why do Conflicts Arise Among Ethnicities?

Learning Outcome 7.3.1: Explain the difference between ethnicity and nationality.

Nationality is identity with a group of people who share legal attachment and personal allegiance to a particular country. Nationalism is loyalty and devotion to a nationality.

Learning Outcome 7.3.2: Identify and describe the principal ethnicities in Lebanon and Sri Lanka.

Lebanon and Sri Lanka are examples of countries where ethnicities have not been able to live in peace.

Learning Outcome 7.3.3: Describe how the Kurds, as well as ethnicities in South Asia, have been divided among more than one nationality.

Some ethnicities find themselves divided among more than one nationality.

Learning Outcome 7.3.4: Identify and describe the principal ethnicities in western Asia.

The lack of correspondence between the territory occupied by ethnicities and nationalities is especially severe in western Asia.

In some countries ethnicities within a state will compete to dominate the national identity of that state. This will often result in civil war. This has been the case in a number of countries in the Horn of Africa. Eritrean rebels fought against the Ethiopian army in the early 1990s and became the independent state of Eritrea in 1993. There has been conflict between the two over the location of the border since that time. There has been civil war in Sudan for decades between the Christian and animist rebels in the south and the Arab-Muslim dominated government forces in the north. Now there is ethnic war in the western-most Darfur region. Somalia is a country in turmoil because of conflict between the six major ethnic groups, known as clans.

In the Middle East Lebanon has experienced civil war because of ethnic and religious divisions. The country is comprised of numerous Christian sects as well as Muslims belonging to both the Shiite and Sunni sects. The island country of Sri Lanka has been torn by fighting between the Sinhalese Buddhists who speak an Indo-European language and the Tamil Hindus who speak a Dravidian language. The long war between the ethnicities ended in 2009 with the defeat of the Tamil.

Conflicts also arise when one ethnicity is split among more than one country. For example there have been major ethnic disputes between India and Pakistan since these countries became independent from Britain in 1947. Even though there was massive forced migration at the time of independence, there are still minorities of Hindus in Pakistan and minorities of Muslims in India. In addition, the two countries never agreed on the location of their boundary in the northern region of Kashmir.

Key Issues Revisited

7.3. Why do conflicts arise among ethnicities?

- Conflicts can develop when a country contains several ethnicities that vie for political control

- Conflicts can also develop when an ethnicity is divided among more than one country

Review Questions

7.3.1. Nationalities share all BUT which of the following?

A. passports

B. voting

C. civic duty

D. religion

E. loyalty

7.3.2. Most Maronite Christians live in

A. Israel.

B. Lebanon.

C. Jordan.

D. Kuwait.

E. Syria.

KEY ISSUE 4

Why Do Ethnicities Engage in Ethnic Cleansing and Genocide?

Learning Outcome 7.4.1: Describe the process of ethnic cleansing.

Ethnic cleansing has been undertaken in recent years in the Balkans.

Learning Outcome 7.4.2: Explain the concept of ethnic cleansing in the Balkans.

Balkanization is a process by which a state breaks down through conflicts among its ethnicities.

Learning Outcome 7.4.3: Identify the principal episodes of genocide in northeastern Africa.

Genocide is the mass killing of a group of people in an attempt to eliminate the entire group from existence.

Learning Outcome 7.4.4: Identify the principal episodes of genocide in central Africa.

Genocide has been practiced in several places in Africa, including Sudan, Somalia, Rwanda, and the Democratic Republic of Congo.

Throughout history conflict between ethnic groups has led to forced migration. **Ethnic cleansing** is the process by which a more powerful ethnic group forcibly removes a less powerful one in order to create their own nation or nation-state. The case of ethnic cleansing in Bosnia and Herzegovina is a classic recent example. Bosnia was the most multiethnic republic of former Yugoslavia. At the time of the breakup of Yugoslavia in the early 1990s the population of Bosnia consisted of 48% Bosnian Muslim, 37% Serb, and 14% Croat. Serbs and Croats fought to unite their ethnicity in Bosnia with their respective republics; this is called **irredentism**. The Serbs in Bosnia were **irredenta** of Serbia. To do this they both engaged in ethnic cleansing of Bosnian Muslims.

After the breakup of Yugoslavia, Serbia remained a multiethnic state. In fact their southern **province** of Kosovo is 90% ethnic Albanian. Serbia launched a campaign of ethnic cleansing of the Albanian majority. Eventually Serbia withdrew its troops from Kosovo as a result of a North Atlantic Treaty Organization (NATO) air attack. Kosovo declared its independence from Serbia in 2008.

The Balkans has always been a region of ethnic conflict. Indeed the term **balkanized** is used to describe a geographic area that cannot be organized into one or more stable states. **Balkanization** is the process by which a state breaks down through ethnic conflict. The region is also referred to as a **shatterbelt** for the same reasons.

Ethnic cleansing led to **genocide** in Rwanda in the 1990s because of longstanding conflict between the Hutus and the Tutsis. The Hutus were farmers and the Tutsis were cattle herders. Historically the Tutsi took control and made the Hutus their serfs. The region was colonized by the Belgians and Germans and shortly before independence in 1962 Hutus killed or ethnically cleansed most of the Tutsis. The 1994 ethnic cleansing and genocide was when Tutsis defeated the Hutu army and killed half a million Hutus. This conflict has spilled into neighboring countries, especially the Democratic Republic of the Congo, and the region is still very unstable because of ethnic conflict.

Key Issues Revisited

7.4. Why do ethnicities engage in ethnic cleansing and genocide?

- Ethnic cleansing is an attempt by one ethnic group to remove all members of another ethnic group in order to create an ethnically homogeneous region

- Ethnic cleansing was practiced in the conflict in Yugoslavia during the 1990s

Review Questions

7.4.1. Which group practiced ethnic cleansing the village of Golane in Kosovo?

A. Macedonians

B. Bosnians

C. Serbians

D. Albanians

E. Slovenians

7.4.2. The janjaweed would most likely be found in what area?

A. Cairo, Egypt

B. Damascus, Syria

C. Beirut, Lebanon

D. Darfur, Sudan

E. Rabat, Morocco

Key Terms

Apartheid
Balkanization
Balkanized
Blockbusting
Centripetal forces
Centrifugal forces
Ethnic cleansing
Ethnic neighborhoods
Ethnicity
Ethnonationalism
Genocide
Ghettos
Irredenta
Irredentism

Multicultural
Multiethnic state
Multinational state
Nationalism
Nationality
Nation-state
Province
Race
Racism
Racist
Self-determination
Sharecropper
Shatterbelt
Triangular slave trade

Think Like a Geographer Activities

http://www.washingtonpost.com/wp-srv/national/longterm/meltingpot/melt0222.htm
If you go to the above link, read the article and attempt to answer the question, "Is America a melting pot even though there is the appearance of ethnic segregation?"

Quick Quiz

7.1. Los Angeles has what kind of ethnic distribution?
A) dispersed
B) clustered
C) diverse
D) contiguous
E) segregated

7.2. Race is
A) characterized by Caucasian, African American, and Hispanic/Latino.
B) self-identification with a group sharing a biological ancestor.
C) determinable from physical characteristics, like DNA.
D) evenly distributed around the world.
E) determined by the country you come from.

7.3. A nation or nationality is
A) a group of people tied to a place through legal status and tradition.
B) a country.
C) ethnic identity.
D) any cohesive group of people.
E) was determined by apartheid laws.

7.4. In the United States, which is shared by all Americans?
A) nationality
B) language
C) ethnicity
D) race
E) DNA

7.5. Nation-states in Europe were formed
A) in the nineteenth century.
B) easily from empire boundaries.
C) by drawing boundaries.
D) and have not changed at all.
E) by the Ottoman Turks.

7.6. Globalization has affected Africa in all but
A) religion.
B) ethnicity.
C) development.
D) urbanization.
E) language.

Free Response

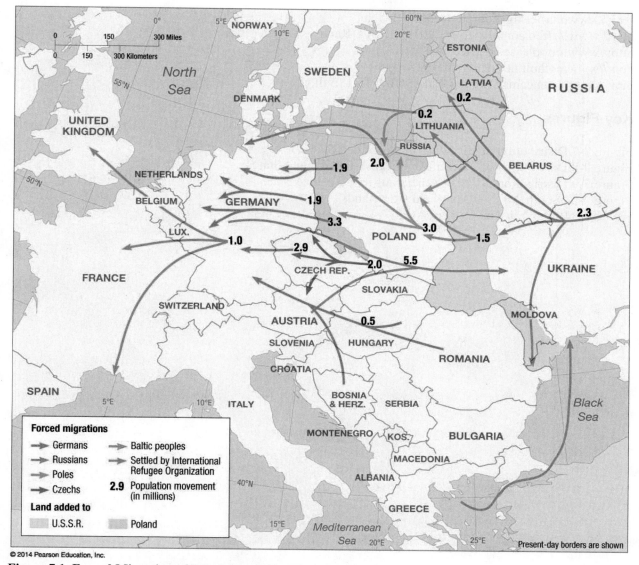

Figure 7.1 Forced Migration of Ethnicities After World War II

A.   Look at the map above (Figure 7-37 in your textbook) and describe the impact of forced migration in Europe in terms of ethnicities and their spatial distributions.

B.   Does this migration impact nationalistic tendency? Give one example.

C.   Describe the implications of multiethnic countries to the concept of nation-states.

On the Web

http://www.masteringgeography.com
http://www.diffen.com/difference/Ethnicity_vs_Race
http://www.infoplease.com/ipa/A0855617.html
http://www.notholt.net/fields_of_fire/
http://www.sciencemag.org/content/336/6083/818.full.pdf

Key Figures

Figure 7-7 Distribution of Hispanics in the United States
Figure 7-8 Distribution of African Americans in the United States
Figure 7-9 Distribution of Asian Americans in the United States
Figure 7-23 South Africa's Apartheid Homelands
Figure 7-34 Ethnicities in Western Asia

Chapter

8 Political Geography

Where Are States Distributed?

This chapter outlines the location of states and the changing face of **geopolitics** since the end of the Cold War. The location of boundaries gives some indication as to potential instability and boundary disputes between countries. States also cooperate with each other, and some countries have transferred military, economic, and political authority to regional and worldwide collections of states. Finally the chapter considers reasons for terrorist attacks, and the relationship between terrorism and political geography.

Leaning Outcome 8.1.1: Explain the three eras of rapid growth in UN membership.

All but a handful of states are members of the UN. UN membership grew rapidly in 1955 when many European states joined, in 1960 when many African states joined, and in the 1990s when states formerly part of the Soviet Union and Yugoslavia joined.

Learning Outcome 8.1.2: Explain why it is difficult to determine whether some territories are states.

Several places are not universally recognized as sovereign states. Polar regions have not been organized into states, although neighboring states have competing claims on them.

Learning Outcome 8.1.3: Explain the concept of nation-state and how it differs from earlier ways to govern.

Dividing the world into a collection of states is a modern concept. Historically, most of Earth's surface was organized in other ways, such as empires, or else unorganized.

The concept of dividing the world into a collection of independent states is relatively recent, dating from eighteenth century Europe, but the concept of territoriality can be traced to the ancient Middle East. The first states in Mesopotamia, which was at the eastern end of the ancient Fertile Crescent, were known as city-states. A **city-state** is a sovereign state that consists of a town or city and the surrounding countryside.

Later the Roman Empire provided the best example of the power of political unity. After the collapse of the Roman Empire in the fifth century A.D. Europe was divided into a large number of feudal estates. Ultimately powerful kings gained control in Western Europe and their kingdoms formed the basis for the development of the modern states that included England, France, and Spain.

Political geography can be studied at a number of different scales, including local, national, and international politics. The fundamental unit of political geography is the country which is formally called a **state**. This is an area organized into a political unit and ruled by an established government that has **sovereignty** over its internal and external affairs. This definition if a state is tested in some places, notably Korea, China and Taiwan, Western Sahara (Sahrawi Republic), and the Polar Regions. North and South Korea were admitted to the United Nations as separate countries but they both have some commitment to reunification. China has claimed Taiwan since the establishment of that country when Nationalists fled there from China in the late 1940s. Morocco still claims Western Sahara although most African countries recognize it as a sovereign state. The Polar Regions are the only large landmasses on Earth's surface that are not part of a state. Antarctica is managed by the Antarctic Treaty (1959), which allows states to establish research stations on the continent. The United Nations Convention on the Law of the Sea (1982) has allowed states to submit claims within the Arctic Circle.

Key Issues Revisited

8.1. Where are states distributed?

- A state is a political unit, with an organized government and sovereignty

- A nation is a group of people with a strong sense of cultural unity

- Most of Earth's surface is allocated to states, and only a few colonies and areas of unorganized territory remain

Review Questions

8.1.1. A state is a good example of what type of region?

A. vernacular

B. functional

C. traditional

D. formal

E. perceived

8.1.2. With the collapse of the Roman Empire, the empire was broken up into

A. colonies.

B. nation-states.

C. estates.

D. city-states.

E. fortified cities.

KEY ISSUE 2

Why Are Nation-States Difficult to Create?

Learning Outcome 8.2.1: Understand the difference between a nation-state and a multinational state. Although there is no perfect nation-state, some states come close.

A multinational state contains multiple ethnicities rather than a single ethnicity.

Learning Outcome 8.2.2: Describe differences among states formerly in the Soviet Union.

The Soviet Union was once the world's largest multinational state.
The country's largest ethnicities were organized into 15 republics that are now independent states.

Learning Outcome 8.2.3: Describe patterns of distribution of ethnicities in Russia and the Caucasus.

Russia is now the world's largest multinational state, with numerous ethnic groups especially in areas that border other states. The Caucasus Mountain region contains a complex array of ethnicities divided among several small states.

Learning Outcome 8.2.4: Explain the concept of colonies and describe their current distribution.

A colony is territory legally tied to a state. Into the twentieth century, much of the world consisted of colonies, but few remain.

A **nation** consists of a group of people with a common ethnic and political identity, but every nation does not have its own state. A **nation-state** is where political boundaries coincide with the territory occupied by a particular ethnicity that has been transformed into a nationality.

The land area occupied by states varies considerably in the world. Russia is the largest state, encompassing 11% of the world's land area. Other large states include China, Canada, the United States, and Brazil. There are also numerous very small states or **microstates**. States such as Monaco and Vatican City, both of which are located within Italy, are good examples of microstates. Larger states usually have more extensive natural resources.

At the international geopolitical level three theories have been important in the development of the nation-state concept in the last two hundred years. In the late nineteenth century Friedrich Ratzel proposed his **organic theory** of the evolution of nations. According to Ratzel, states that did not expand their land area would disintegrate like an organism that fails to find food. Sir Halford Mackinder developed his **heartland theory** at the beginning of the twentieth century. He believed that the Eurasian landmass was the world's heartland and thus the key to world domination. Nicholas Spykman disagreed, and argued the rimland area surrounding the heartland and including the world's oceans was the key to world political power; this was his **rimland theory.**

European states controlled much of the world through **colonialism** beginning in the early 1500s. They established **colonies** by imposing their political, economic, and cultural control (especially religion) on territories in Latin America, Asia, and Africa that became legally tied to them. Some states that remained independent became **buffer states**, separating areas of colonial control. For example, Thailand became a buffer state between British India and French Indochina. Technically colonialism refers to the control of territory previously uninhabited, whereas **imperialism** is the control of territory that is already occupied, but the two terms are used interchangeably.

Latin American countries became independent in the first half of the nineteenth century, and **decolonization** proceeded rapidly across Africa and Asia after World War II. Today there are only a few remaining colonies, and these are generally only very small territories around the globe.

Key Issues Revisited

8.2. Why are nation-states difficult to create?

- Usually boundaries are drawn to coincide with physical features, such as mountains, deserts, and bodies of water, or with cultural characteristics such as geometry, religion, and language

Review Questions

8.2.1. The official language of Greenland is

A. Danish.

B. Slovenian.

C. Serbian.

D. Turkish.

E. Greenlandic.

8.2.2. The countries that make up the Caucasus Region include

A. Russia, Armenia, and Georgia.

B. Latvia, Lithuania, and Estonia.

C. Armenia, Azerbaijan, and Georgia.

D. Estonia, Armenia, and Russia.

E. Armenia, Georgia, and Kazakhstan.

KEY ISSUE 3

Why Do Boundaries Cause Problems?

Learning Outcome 8.3.1: Describe the types of physical boundaries between states.

Physical features used to delineate boundaries include deserts, mountains, and bodies of water.

Learning Outcome 8.3.2: Describe the types of cultural boundaries between states.

Geometry and ethnicities can be used to delineate cultural boundaries between states.

Learning Outcome 8.3.3: Describe five shapes of states.

States take five forms: compact, elongated, prorupted, perforated, and fragmented. Landlocked states have no access to the sea.

Learning Outcome 8.3.4: Describe differences among the three regime types.

Regimes can be democratic, anocratic, or autocratic; the trend has been toward more democratic regimes. Local governments can be organized according to unitary or federal state principles; the trend has been toward more federal states.

Learning Outcome 8.3.5: Explain the concept of gerrymandering and three ways that it is done.

Gerrymandering is the redrawing of electoral districts to benefit the party in power. Three forms of gerrymandering are wasted vote, excess vote, and stacked vote.

State (or territorial) morphology, or the shape of a state determines the length of its boundaries with other states, as well as potential communication and conflict with neighboring states.

Countries like Poland that are relatively rounded are **compact states**. This shape enhances communications between all regions, especially when the capital is centrally located.

Prorupted states are compact states with a large projecting extension. Proruptions can disrupt, like the Afghanistan proruption which denies Russia a shared boundary with Pakistan. They can also provide access such as Namibia's proruption, which was originally designed to give this former German colony access to the Zambezi River in southwest Africa.

Elongated states, such as Chile and The Gambia, are long and thin. Such states often suffer from poor internal communications.

A state that is divided into several discontinuous pieces of territory is called a **fragmented state**. The United States is fragmented because Alaska is separated from the contiguous lower 48 states. Kaliningrad is separated from the rest of Russia by the independent states of Lithuania and Belarus. Island states like Indonesia are fragmented because of water. In addition some states have fragmented territory that lies completely within the boundary of another state. This was the case with West Berlin during the Cold War and is called an **exclave**. The boundary between East and West Berlin as well as the boundary between East and West Germany is now a **relic boundary** because it no longer exists. An **enclave** is a piece of territory that is surrounded by another political unit of which it is not a part. Lesotho is an enclave because it is completely surrounded by South Africa.

States like Italy and South Africa that completely surround other states are known as **perforated states**. The states that are completely surrounded, such as Lesotho by South Africa, are also **landlocked states** that lack access to the ocean or a sea.

The various shapes of states provide both advantages and disadvantages. Some states occupy strategically important locations on Earth's surface. This is true of Singapore on the tip of Malaysia in Southeast Asia and Panama on the isthmus between North and South America.

Borders, called boundaries, separate states from each other. A boundary is an invisible line that completely surrounds a state, marks the outer limits of its territorial control, and gives it a distinctive shape. Prior to the establishment of formal boundaries, **frontiers** separated states. A frontier is a zone or area between states where no state exercises complete control. Frontiers do still exist between states on the Arabian Peninsula where the borders are virtually uninhabited desert regions.

Physical boundaries follow important physical features on the landscape, such as water, mountains, and deserts. For example, the boundary between France and Spain is the crest of the Pyrenees Mountains, and the boundary separating Uganda, Kenya, and Tanzania runs through Lake Victoria.

Physical boundaries are often **antecedent boundaries** because they were natural boundaries long before those areas became populated.

There are a number of different types of **cultural boundaries** between states. **Geometric boundaries** follow straight lines and have little to do with the physical or cultural landscape. The boundaries between many African states today are geometric. They are also called **superimposed boundaries** because they were drawn by European colonial powers that did not pay any attention to the social, cultural, or ethnic compositions of African people.

When British India became independent in 1948, the boundary that was created between the newly independent states of India and Pakistan was essentially a **religious boundary**. It separated a predominantly Muslim Pakistan from a predominantly Hindu India. It is also a superimposed boundary in that it was drawn long after the area had been settled and had established itself.

Language boundaries have always been important cultural boundaries between ethnic groups. This has been especially true in Western Europe for centuries and is becoming increasingly important in Southern and Eastern Europe.

There are now accepted **maritime boundaries** in the world's oceans. As a result of the **United Nations Convention on the Law of the Sea (UNCLOS),** each state with an ocean boundary has a 12 mile **territorial sea**, and a 200 mile **Exclusive Economic Zone (EEZ)** over which it has certain economic rights. Where the water distance between two countries is less than 24 miles, sometimes called **choke points, median lines** delimit the boundary between the two countries equidistant from each shore. **Delimitation** refers to the actual creation of a boundary as a cartographic representation. Beyond this 200 mile limit lie the **high seas** that are beyond national jurisdiction, and are free and open for all countries to use.

Territorial conflict often occurs if a state contains more than one ethnic group. A **multinational state** contains two or more ethnic groups. The island of Cyprus contains two ethnic groups, Greek and Turkish. The two nationalities are geographically separated on the island by a **demarcation** zone created by the United Nations. The former Soviet Union was the largest multinational state in the world, and contained 15 republics that are now independent states. Russia is still the largest multinational state because there are still ethnic groups within Russia, like Chechnya, that are fighting for **self-determination** or the right to become an independent state. Thus in spite of greater global political cooperation, local diversity has increased in political affairs and individual ethnic groups are demanding more control over territory. The pressures for independence within a multinational state from various ethnic groups are also known as **devolution** or **devolutionary pressures**. These pressures are also referred to as **centrifugal forces** because they pull countries apart.

Conflict can also occur where an ethnic group is divided among more than one state. In the Caucasus region there are minorities of Armenia in Azerbaijan and vice versa. The Kurds are a **stateless** ethnic group split among these two states as well as four others in the region.

Political geographers have identified four major types of boundary disputes between states. **Definitional boundary disputes** are over the legal language of a boundary agreement. **Locational boundary disputes** focus on issues related to the delimitation and demarcation of the boundary. **Operational boundary disputes** are conflicts dealing with the operation or functioning of a boundary, and **allocational boundary disputes** are usually over conflicts about resources at the boundary, especially where the boundary is at sea.

The governments of states are generally organized in one of two ways. **Unitary states** place most power in the hands of the central government and work best in relatively small nation-states. The best examples of unitary states are those of Western Europe such as Britain and France. **Centripetal forces**, such as the reliance on a strong central government, strong national institutions, and a sense of common history, bind countries together.

Federal states allocate significant power to the units of local government and work well in multinational states where there is potential ethnic conflict. The United States is a federal state, not so much because of ethnic conflict but because of its sheer geographic size. In recent years there has been a global trend toward federal government. Both France and Poland have moved from a unitary toward a federal system in the last few years.

The boundaries separating legislative districts in the United States and other countries have to be redrawn from time to time in order to account for changing population. For example the 435 districts of the U.S. House of Representatives are redrawn after the census every 10 years. This is called **reapportionment** or **redistricting.** In most U.S. states this is done by the state legislature, and historically the political party in control has tried to do this. The redrawing of legislative boundaries to benefit a specific political party in power is called **gerrymandering**. The term was named for Elbridge Gerry, a nineteenth century politician from Massachusetts who tried to do this in his state, and created an oddly shaped district that looked like a salamander that his opponents called a "gerrymander."

There are three types of gerrymandering. "Wasted votes" spreads opposition supporters across many districts. "excess votes" concentrates opposition in few districts, and "stacked votes" links distant areas of similar voters through oddly shaped boundaries. Although the Supreme Court has ruled gerrymandering illegal, stacked vote gerrymandering is still a reality.

Key Issues Revisited

8.3. Why do boundaries cause problems?

- Boundaries affect the shape of countries and affect the ability of a country to live peacefully with its neighbors

- Problems arise when the boundaries of states do not coincide with the boundaries of ethnicities

Review Questions

8.3.1. According to the Law of the Sea, the territorial limits for most countries is

A. 3.5 nautical miles.

B. 12 nautical miles.

C. 3.5 land miles.

D. 5.5 kilometers.

E. 158 miles.

8.3.2. Most landlocked states would be found in

A. Asia.

B. Europe.

C. South America.

D . Africa.

E. the Middle East.

KEY ISSUE 4

Why Do States Cooperate and Compete with Each Other?

Learning Outcome 8.4.1: Describe the principal alliances in Europe during the Cold War era.

During the second half of the twentieth century, relations among states were dominated by the Cold War. States were allied with the two superpowers, the Soviet Union and the United States.

Learning Outcome 8.4.2: Describe the principal economic alliances in Europe in the period since World War II.

With the end of the Cold War, economic alliances have replaced military alliances in importance, especially in Europe.

Learning Outcome 8.4.3: Explain the concept of terrorism.

Terrorism is the systematic use of violence to intimidate a population or coerce a government. Terrorism against the United States culminated in the 9/11 attacks.

Learning Outcome 8.4.4: Describe ways that states have sponsored terrorism.

States have supported terrorism by providing sanctuary to terrorists, supplying them with weapons and intelligence, and planning state-sponsored attacks.

One of the most important trends in international politics is the development of international and regional alliances. **International organizations** are alliances of two or more countries seeking cooperation. The **United Nations** (UN) and the **North American Free Trade Agreement** (NAFTA) are both examples of international alliances. The UN is a global organization that focuses on peace and security whereas NAFTA is a regional economic alliance. The **European Union** (EU) is also a regional economic union, but it also includes elements of political unity. All of these organizations are **supranational organizations** that include the membership of two or more states that relinquish some degree of sovereignty for the benefits of an alliance with other states.

When a large number of states were of roughly equal strength, no single state could dominate. This was the geopolitical situation in Europe before the First World War where European states formed opposing alliances and a **balance of power** was maintained. This changed after the Second World War when the **Warsaw Pact** and the **North Atlantic Treaty Organization** (NATO) became the opposing military alliances of the Cold War. Balance of power became bipolar. Most East European countries were controlled by the Soviet Union during the Cold War and were known as **satellite states**. **Confederations** are similar to international organizations in that they bring several states together for a common purpose. The **Commonwealth of Independent States** (CIS), a confederacy of independent states of the former Soviet Union for common economic and administrative needs, is an example if such an alliance. There are numerous other regional organizations in the world that combine political, military, and economic goals. Other prominent regional organizations include the **Organization on Security and Cooperation in Europe** (OSCE), the **Organization of American States** (OAS), the **African Union** (AU), and the **Commonwealth**.

Terrorism is the systematic use of violence by a group in order to intimidate a population or coerce a government into granting its demands. It is sometimes hard to distinguish terrorism from other acts of political violence. This is the case with some of the actions of the Palestinians against Israel, and Chechen rebels against Russia.

There have been a number of terrorist attacks against the United States in recent years but the most dramatic and devastating was on September 11, 2001. Al-Qaeda has been implicated in many of these attacks including the September 11, 2001, attack. Founded by Osama bin Laden, al-Qaeda consists of numerous cells, unites jihad fighters, and has used fundamentalist Islam to justify attacks, especially against the United States.

Several states in the Middle East have also provided support for terrorism at three levels. Some have provided sanctuary for terrorists wanted by other countries. They have supplied weapons, money, and intelligence to terrorists, and some countries have planned attacks using terrorists. These countries have included Libya, Afghanistan, Iraq, and Iran at various times in recent years.

Key Issues Revisited

8.4. Why do states cooperate and compete with each other?

- After the Second World War, the United States and the Soviet Union, the world's two superpowers, formed military alliances with other countries

- Now that the Cold War has ended, nationalities are cooperating with each other, especially in Western Europe, primarily to promote economic growth rather than to provide military protection

- Terrorism initiated by individuals, organizations, and states has increased, especially against the United States

Review Questions

8.4.1. The main purpose of the European Union is to

A. promote human rights.

B. punish war criminals.

C. provide military aid.

D. stop rebellions in former colonies.

E. promote economic and political cooperation.

8.4.2. Which of these countries is NOT part of the Commonwealth of Nations?

A. Canada

B. Bangladesh

C. Mexico

D. Nigeria

E. Australia

Key Terms

African Union (AU)
Allocational boundary disputes
Antecedent boundaries
Balance of power
Boundary
Buffer state
Centrifugal forces
Centripetal forces
Choke point
City-state
Colonialism
Colonies
Commonwealth
Commonwealth of Independent States (CIS)
Compact state
Confederation
Cultural boundaries
Decolonization
Definitional boundary disputes
Delimitation
Demarcation
Devolution
Elongated state
Enclave
European Union (EU)
Exclave
Exclusive Economic Zone (EEZ)
Federal states
Fragmented state
Frontier
Geometric boundaries
Geopolitics
Gerrymandering
Heartland theory
High seas
Imperialism
International organizations
Landlocked
Locational boundary disputes

Maritime boundaries
Median lines
Microstates
Multinational state
Nation
Nation-state
North American Free Trade Association (NAFTA)
North Atlantic Treaty Organization (NATO)
Operational boundary disputes Organic theory
Organization of American States (OAS)
Organization on Security and Cooperation in Europe (OSCE)
Perforated state
Physical boundaries
Prorupted state
Reapportionment
Redistricting
Relic boundary
Religious boundaries
Rimland theory
Satellite states
Self-determination
Sovereignty
State
Stateless
State morphology
Subsequent boundaries
Superimposed boundaries
Supranational organizations
Territorial sea
Terrorism
Unitary state
United Nations (UN)
United Nations Convention on the Law of the Sea (UNCLOS)
Warsaw Pact

Think Like a Geographer Activities

DATA ACQUISITON CHART FOR ANALYZING NATO AND THE EU

	NATO	EU
Purposes and Principles		
Political Functions		
Economic Functions		
Admissions Issues		
Major Successes		
Failures, Problems and Critical Issues		

What are the major similarities and differences between NATO and the EU?

Write a **Critique of NATO and the EU** for the Council of Europe, comparing the purpose and role played by each of these organizations in postwar Europe. Your critique should include an analysis of the spatial development of these organizations and address the political and economic functions of both NATO and EU as they relate to cooperation and conflict in Europe.

Quick Quiz

Fill in the blank.

8.1. _____ was divided at the 38th parallel in after World War II and even though it was one state, it now is recognized in the UN as two different countries.

8.2. The only landmass on Earth's surface that is not part of a country is the _____.

8.3. A _____ is a state whose territory is occupied by an identifiable ethnic group.

8.4. Of the Baltic States, _____ is the one which most closely represents a nation-state.

8.5. The two types of cultural boundaries are _____ and _____.

8.6. The state shape that tends to have poor internal communications is _____ states.

8.7. An _____ is a state that is neither fully democratic nor autocratic.

8.8. The process of redrawing voting boundaries to help one party is known as _____.

Free Response

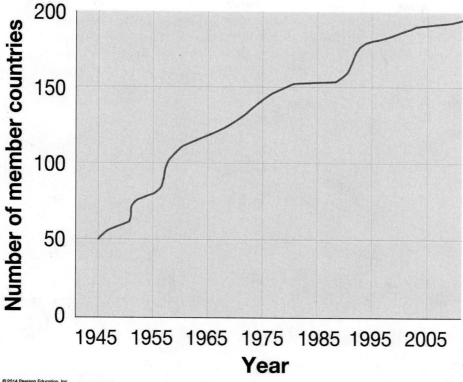

© 2014 Pearson Education, Inc.

Figure 8-1 Growth in UN Membership

1. Identify and explain the three periods in history where the United Nations membership has grown.
2. Discuss one positive outcome of this growth.

On the Web

Here are some useful websites for this chapter:
http://www.masteringgeography.com
http://www.sheppardsoftware.com/Geography.htm
http://geographyworldonline.com/
http://geography.about.com/od/politicalgeography/Political_Geography.htm
http://www.politicalgeography.org/links.html
http://www.un.org/en/

Key Figures

Figure 8-3 UN Members
Figure 8-13 Nation-States in Europe, 1800 and 1924
Figure 8-17 States in the Former U.S.S.R.
Figure 8-23 Colonial Possessions, 1914
Figure 8-34 Regime Type

Chapter

9 Development

Why Does Development Vary among Countries?

The chapter identifies the location of more and less developed countries and then explains why some regions are more developed than others. Obviously less developed countries face much greater obstacles to development. More and less developed regions are distinguished by economic, social, and demographic indicators. Level of development varies according to gender.

Learning Outcome 9.1.1: Describe the HDI standard of living factor.

Standard of living is measured through gross national income per capita at purchasing power parity. Other measures of standard of living include economic structure, productivity, and availability of consumer goods.

Learning Outcome 9.1.2: Describe the HDI health factor.

The HDI health factor is life expectancy at birth.

Learning Outcome 9.1.3: Describe the HDI access to knowledge factor.

The HDI knowledge factors are years of schooling and expected years of schooling. Other measures of access to knowledge include pupil/teacher ratio and literacy rate.

The United Nations HDI identifies gross national income as its economic indicator of development. Other economic indicators that help to distinguish between levels of development include economic structure, purchasing power, worker productivity, access to raw materials and availability of consumer goods. GNI is the value of all goods and services produced in a country, including money that leaves the country. The annual per capita GNI in 2011 exceeded $34,000 in developed countries and was about

$7,000 in developing countries, and this gap has been widening. It is not a perfect measure of economic development because people in many developing countries still operate in largely nonmonetary economies, and it measures average wealth rather than distribution.

The percentage of workers in the different sectors of the economy will help to show the level of development of a country. Workers in the **primary sector** of the economy extract materials from Earth, usually through agriculture. The share of GDP accounted for by the primary sector has decreased in LDCs, but it remains higher than in MDCs. The **secondary sector** is the industrial sector of the economy, and the **tertiary sector** is the service sector of the economy; in MDCs, employment in the secondary sector has decreased. The share of GDP accounted for by the tertiary sector is relatively large in MDCs. Quaternary sector jobs include business services and wholesaling, and quinary sector jobs are in health, education, research, government, retailing, and tourism. However the current practice is to consider all these jobs as groups within the tertiary sector.

Productivity is the value of a particular product compared to the amount of labor needed to make it. It can be measured by the **value added** per worker, which in manufacturing is the gross value of the product minus the costs of raw materials and energy. Productivity is much higher in MDCs because of higher technology and capital intensive industries. Production in LDCs is still very labor intensive.

Development requires access to raw materials, although some developed countries such as Japan, Singapore, and Switzerland lack significant resources; some developing countries such as those in sub-Saharan Africa have significant raw materials. Development also requires energy to fuel industry and transform raw materials into finished products.

Countries that produce more quality nonessential consumer goods are able to promote expansion of industry and the generation of additional wealth. Consumer goods such as automobiles, telephones, and televisions are very accessible to many people in MDCs but only to the few who are wealthy in LDCs.

Education and health are key social indicators of development. High levels of development are associated with high levels of education. The quality of education is typically measured by student/teacher ratio and literacy rates. The **literacy rate** is the percentage of a country's population who can read and write. Literacy rates in MDCs usually exceed 99%, whereas many LDCs have rates that are below 70%. There are also huge differences between literacy rates for men and women in developing countries. People are also healthier in more developed countries because they have better nutrition and access to health care.

The United Nations' HDI includes life expectancy as a measure of development. Other demographic indicators include infant mortality, natural increase, and crude birth rates. Life expectancy is a measure of health and welfare; some developed countries have life expectancies that are twice as high as developing countries. Infant mortality rates speak to levels of health care in a country. Rates of natural increase are much higher in LDCs and force them to allocate increasing percentages of their GDP's to care for a rapidly expanding population. Developing countries have higher rates of natural increase because they have higher crude birth rates. One has to be careful when looking at crude death rates to help measure levels of development for two reasons. Firstly the diffusion of medical technology from MDCs to LDCs has reduced death rates in less developed countries. Secondly the high crude death rates of some MDCs are a reflection of their higher percentages of elderly and lower percentages of children.

Development is the process of economic growth, where countries try to improve their level of material wealth through the diffusion and realization of resources, knowledge, and technology. It is a continuous process and each country lies somewhere along that continuum. A **more developed country (MDC** and also known as a **developed country)** will be further along that continuum than a **less developed country (LDC** and also known as a **developing country)**.

The **Human Development Index (HDI)** is one measure of development. It was created by the United Nations and calculates development in terms of human welfare rather than money or productivity. It evaluates human welfare in three areas: economic, social, and demographic. The economic factor is **gross domestic product** per capita (GDP); the social factors are the **literacy rate** and amount of education; and the demographic factor is life expectancy. The highest HDI possible is 1.0 or 100% and the countries of the world can be categorized into nine regions according to their level of development.

Five of the nine regions identified by the United Nations HDI are more developed. These include

North America, Europe, Russia, Japan, and the Oceania. North America has the highest HDI (0.95) and is well endowed with natural resources and agricultural land. It has developed high-tech industries, and is a leading consumer and the world's largest market. Its high percentage of tertiary sector employment has offset the loss of manufacturing.

During the Cold War Europe was regarded as two regions. With the fall of communism, the two parts of Europe have become much closer. Europe has a very high HDI (0.94). Europe has become the world's largest and richest market with the elimination of most economic barriers through the European Union. Levels of development are highest in western and northern Europe. Europe is dependent on international trade and, to pay for imports, it produces high-value goods and services. The recent recession has exacerbated regional and national differences. Unemployment has been particularly severe in Southern and Eastern Europe.

Russia struggled to transition to a market economy after the dissolution of the Soviet Union in 1991, and its HDI actually declined. It has now experienced a few years of growth and now has an HDI of 0.81. However the severe worldwide recession caused a sharp drop in demand, and its HDI could decline again.

Japan has become a great economic power despite lacking key resources. It has developed a skilled labor force that specializes in high-quality and high-value products. Japan has an HDI of 0.96. Australia and New Zealand share many cultural characteristics with Britain although their economies, which are net exporters of food and other resources, are increasingly tied to Asian countries. Oceania has an HDI of 0.86.

The six regions that can be classified as less developed include Latin America, East Asia, Central Asia, Southwest Asia and North Africa, Southeast Asia, South Asia, and sub-Saharan Africa in order of development level.

A higher percentage of people in Latin America, with an HDI of 0.81, live in urban areas than any other developing region. Development in this region is also characterized by tremendous inequality in income distribution. In East Asia, which has an HDI of 0.76, China is now the world's second largest economy, and the largest market for consumer products. Manufacturing has moved to this region because of low wages, which is driving down factory pay around the world. There are also regional economic equalities in China.

Most of the countries of Central Asia were once part of the Soviet Union. Levels of development in Kazakhstan and Iran are relatively high, especially because of petroleum production. In the other republics minerals and agricultural products are the main economic resources. Afghanistan probably has one of the world's lowest HDIs. The region's HDI is 0.75.

The harsh physical environment of Southwest Asia and North Africa, with an HDI of 0.67, does not support high population concentrations but the region has the largest percentage of the world's petroleum reserves. This allows many countries in the region to enjoy a trade surplus and use petroleum wealth to finance economic development. However, there is a large gap in per capita income between the petroleum-rich countries and those that lack resources. These countries have to deal with traditional cultural values associated with Islam which can hinder development, especially where the role of women is concerned. The region suffers from serious internal cultural disputes. Southwest Asia has also struggled with terrorism.

Indonesia, Vietnam, and Thailand are the most populous countries in Southeast Asia (HDI of 0.72), a region that concentrates on the production of agricultural products that are used in manufacturing. Some countries in this region, including Thailand, Singapore, Malaysia, and the Philippines, have developed rapidly especially because of growing manufacturing built on cheap labor. Economic growth in the region has slowed since the last years of the twentieth century. South Asia (HDI of 0.59) has the second-highest population and the second-lowest per capita income. India is one of the world's leading rice and wheat producers thanks in large part to the innovations of the Green Revolution. It now has the world's fourth largest economy.

With an HDI of 0.47, sub-Saharan Africa is the poorest region in the world, although it is a major source of mineral wealth. Many of the region's economic and political problems are legacies of the colonial era.

The tropical and dry climates of the region are not capable of supporting large concentrations of people, but sub-Saharan Africa has the highest rate of natural increase in the world.

Key Issues Revisited

9.1. Why does development vary among countries?

- Development is the process by which the material conditions of a country's people are improved

- An MDC has a higher level of per capita GDP as a result of the structural transformation of the economy from an agricultural to a service-providing society.

- MDCs use their wealth to provide better health, education, and welfare services, whereas LDCs must use their additional wealth largely to meet the most basic needs of a rapidly growing population

- The five regions of MDCs include Europe, North America, Japan, Oceania, and Russia

- The seven regions of LDCs are Latin America, East Asia, Central Asia, Southwest Asia, Southeast Asia, South Asia, and sub-Saharan Africa

Review Questions

9.1.1. Countries with the lowest HDI would be found in what region?

A. Southeast Asia

B. Central Asia

C. Europe

D. Sub-Saharan Africa

E. Latin America

9.1.2. Over 60% of jobs in MDCs would be in what sector of the economy?

A. tertiary

B. secondary

C. primary

D. agricultural

E. none of these is correct

KEY ISSUE 2

Why Does Development Vary by Gender?

Learning Outcome 9.2.1: Describe the UN's measures of gender inequality.

The GII measures the extent of gender inequality. The GII combines measures of empowerment, labor force participation, and reproductive rights.

Learning Outcome 9.2.2: Describe changes since the 1990s in gender inequality.

Gender inequality has declined in most countries since 1990, although not in the United States.

The **Gender Inequality Index (GII)** combines multiple measures, including empowerment and labor and reproductive health. A country with complete gender equality would have a GII of 0. A country with a high GII means that there is a great amount of disparity between men and women. The lowest GIIs are found in countries that have a high HDI.   The empowerment measure of GII looks at the degree of education and political power held by women. The economic indicator is the percentage of women who have completed high school. This indicator is much higher in MDCs than in LDCs. One indicator of the political power of women is the percentage of the country's administrative and managerial jobs they hold. This is higher in MDCs, especially Europe, than LDCs. The other political indicator of empower-ment is the percentage of women elected to public office. Key indicators look better for LDCs now than a generation ago, but the gap in key development indicators between LDCs and MDCs remains wide.

Key Issues Revisited

9.2. Why does development vary by gender?

- The United Nations has found evidence of gender inequality in every country of the world

- Women have lower levels of income, literacy, and education than men

- Even in countries where women have achieved near-equality with men, they still have much less economic and political power

Review Questions

9.2.1. The lowest rate of female participation in the work force would be found in

A. Eastern Europe.

B. Central Asia.

C. Southwest Asia.

D. Latin America.

E. North America.

9.2.2. According to the UN, gender inequality adversely affects which of these?

A. the environment

B. politics

C. childbirth

D. life expectancy

E. death rates

KEY ISSUE 3

Why are Energy Resources Important for Development?

Learning Outcome 9.3.1: Explain the principal sources of demand for fossil fuels.

Most energy is supplied by three fossil fuels: coal, petroleum, and natural gas. Developed countries and developing countries each consume approximately half of the world's energy.

Learning Outcome 9.3.2: Describe the distribution of production of the three fossil fuels.

Fossil fuels are not distributed uniformly around the world, and they are nonrenewable sources of energy.

Learning Outcome 9.3.3: Describe the distribution of reserves of fossil fuels and the difference between proven and potential reserves.

Reserves are divided into proven (in fields already discovered) and potential (fields thought to exist). Proven reserves are not distributed uniformly.

Learning Outcome 9.3.4: Describe the role of OPEC and changes in the price and availability of petroleum.

Much of the world's petroleum reserves are located in countries that belong to OPEC. The United States has increased its dependence on petroleum imported from neighbors in the Western Hemisphere.

Learning Outcome 9.3.5: Describe the distribution of nuclear energy and challenges in using it.

Nuclear is the principal source of energy other than the three fossil fuels in the United States and a couple dozen other countries.

Numerous problems limit the use of nuclear power, including threat of accidents, disposal of waste, use in making weapons, limited reserves, and high costs.

Humans and animals supply animate power. Since the Industrial Revolution there has been a tremendous increase in **inanimate power,** which is generated by machines. Three **fossil fuels,** oil, natural gas, and coal, provide five-sixths of the world's energy. In some LDCs **biomass fuel,** such as wood, plant material, and animal waste, is still the major source of fuel.

Fossil fuels are examples of **nonrenewable energy.** Remaining supplies are **proven reserves** and **potential reserves.** The world's proven reserves of natural gas will last for about 49 years, which is slightly more than petroleum reserves and much less than coal reserves.

New technology can make potential reserves a reality but extraction is now much harder. New fields may yet be discovered, and unconventional sources may be developed.

Fossil fuels are unevenly distributed around the globe. China extracts 39% of the world's coal, and the United States extracts 16%. Australia, India, Russia, and South Africa also all have major reserves. Saudi Arabia, Iran, Iraq, Kuwait, and the United Arab Emirates, all of which are members of the **Organization of Petroleum Exporting Countries (OPEC),** have 60 % of the world's oil reserves. Russia and the United States each account for one-fourth of world natural gas production. A few LDCs in Africa, Asia, and Latin America have extensive reserves of one or more fossil fuels, but most have little. MDCs currently consume about three-quarters of the world's energy although LDCs, especially China, are beginning to consume more as they become developed.

Nuclear power is becoming an increasing energy source, and it now supplies about one-sixth of the world's electricity. The world's leading generators of nuclear power are the United States, France, and Japan. A nuclear power plant produces electricity from energy released by splitting uranium atoms in a process called **fission**. Problems associated with nuclear power include potential accidents, **radioactive waste**, generation of plutonium, a limited uranium supply, geographic distribution, and cost. **Nuclear fusion** could address some of the issues associated with nuclear power. It fuses hydrogen atoms to form helium but can only occur at very high temperatures. Thus fusion has not yet been successfully used to generate power.

Minerals are plentiful on Earth's surface and are potential resources if people can find a use for them. Minerals are either metallic or nonmetallic. Nonmetallic metals include various stones and sand, as well as nitrogen, phosphorus, and other sources of fertilizer. Metallic minerals are ferrous, derived from iron, or **nonferrous**, of which the most abundant is aluminum.

The leading **renewable resources** are biomass and hydroelectric power. **Biomass, geothermal energy**, and **wind power** are also becoming important. Biomass energy comes from wood and crops. Windmills in wind farms create wind energy. Geothermal energy is generated from hot water or steam in volcanic areas, especially Iceland. Wood and plants are important forms of biomass that are renewable resources if they are carefully harvested. The energy of moving water has been used to generate **hydroe-lectric power**, which is the second most important source of electricity after coal, supplying about one-fourth of the world's demand. The biggest drawback with hydroelectric power is that the building of dams that can cause serious environmental damage often generates it.

Solar energy is free and **ubiquitous**, and thus potentially the most important renewable resource. It can be harnessed either through passive or active means. **Passive solar energy systems** capture solar energy without any special devices, whereas **active solar energy systems** collect solar energy and convert it to heat energy or electricity. In direct electric conversion, solar radiation is captured with **photo-voltaic cells**, which convert light energy to electrical energy.

Key Issues Revisited

9.3. Why is energy important for development?

- Consumption of resources results in depletion

- Fossil fuels and mineral are distributed unevenly across the Earth's surface, and supplies are not found in places where demand is highest

- Converting from nonrenewable to renewable sources of energy can minimize depletion and destruction of scarce resources

Review Questions

9.3.1. The leading energy source in the United States and Europe in 1880 was

A. wood

B. natural gas

C. kerosene

D. coal

E. solar

9.3.2. The leading consumer of energy is

A. India.

B. China.

C. the United States.

D. England.

E. France.

KEY ISSUE 4

Why Do Countries Face Obstacles to Development?

Learning Outcome 9.3.6: Describe challenges to increasing the use of alternative energy sources.

Leading renewable energy sources include biomass, hydroelectric, geothermal, wind, and solar.

Learning Outcome 9.3.7: Describe the difference between passive and active solar energy.

Active solar energy captures energy with special devices, such as photovoltaic cells, whereas passive solar energy does not.

Learning Outcome 9.4.1: Summarize the two paths to development.

To promote development, developing countries choose either the self-sufficiency path or the international trade path.

Learning Outcome 9.4.2: Describe shortcomings of the two development paths and reasons international trade has triumphed.

Self-sufficiency has protected inefficient businesses.

Learning Outcome 9.4.3: Identify the main sources of financing development

Finance comes from direct investment by transnational corporations and loans form banks and international organizations.

Learning Outcome 9.4.4: Explain problems with financing development in developing and developed countries.
Developing countries have been required to adopt structural adjustment programs.

Developed countries have had to choose between policies that promote short-term growth and those that promote austerity.

Learning Outcome 9.4.5: Explain the principles of fair trade.

Fair trade attempts to protect workers and small businesses in developing countries.
Fair trade involves a combination of producer and worker standards.

Learning Outcome 9.4.6: Describe ways in which differences in development have narrowed or stayed wide.

Developing countries have closed the gap with developed countries in some respects, such as health, but not in other respects, such as income.

For much of the twentieth century, self-sufficiency or balanced growth was the most popular development alternative, especially for LDCs. It protects infant industries by setting barriers and tariffs on imports, as well as fixing quotas and requiring licenses to restrict the number of legal importers. India followed this model of development in the decades after independence from Britain. It has two major problems. It protects inefficient industries and creates a large bureaucracy to administer the various controls.

Development through international trade takes a very different approach. By following this approach a country can develop its unique economic assets and use the funds from these exports to finance other development.

In the 195's W.W. Rostow proposed his **development model**, which helped countries to move towards development through international trade. This was a five-stage model. Stage one was a traditional society where a country was still predominantly agricultural. In stage two a country reaches the preconditions for takeoff when entrepreneurs initiate economic activities. Infrastructure develops and productivity increases. Stage three is takeoff, which is essentially the beginning of an industrial revolution. In the drive to maturity stage industry diffuses and results in rapid growth. According to Rostow the final stage is the age of mass consumption, when the economy shifts from heavy industry to the production of consumer goods. This model was based on the belief that MDCs in Western Europe and Anglo-America would be followed by countries in Eastern Europe and Japan. Also, many LDCs have an abundance of raw materials that would generate funds to promote development in these countries.

Richard Nolan's **stages of growth model** is similar to Rostow's model. It has six stages but focuses more on increased technology as a society develops.

The international trade approach has been followed by numerous countries in Asia. The most successful initially in Asia included South Korea, Singapore, Taiwan, and Hong Kong (then a British colony). They concentrated on the production of manufacturing goods using cheap labor. The petroleum-rich Arab countries pursued the same approach. Saudi Arabia, Kuwait, Bahrain, Oman, and the United Arab Emirates have been very successful, using petroleum revenues to finance large-scale projects.

The international trade approach to development also has problems. These include uneven resource distribution, market stagnation, and increased dependence on MDCs. But it has now been embraced by most countries. This approach has been aided by the creation of the **World Trade Organization (WTO)** in 1995, which helps to reduce barriers to international trade. The WTO helps to eliminate trade restrictions between countries. It also enforces international trade agreements.

Investment made by **transnational corporations (TNCs)** in foreign countries is known as **foreign direct investment (FDI)**. Of the 500 largest TNCs in 2008, 153 had headquarters in the United States in 2005 and 189 in Europe.

LDCs borrow money for major projects from two major international lenders. The **World Bank** includes the International Bank for Reconstruction and Development (IBRD) and the International Development Association (IDA). They provide loans for the reform of public administration and legal institutions. The **International Monetary Fund (IMF)** provides loans to countries that have balance-of-payment problems rather than for specific projects. There are numerous problems associated with all of these loans. Many new projects in LDCs are expensive failures, and many LDCs have been unable to repay interest and loans. Neither of these organizations will cancel or refinance debts without strings attached. Before granting debt relief, an LDC is required to prepare a Policy Framework Paper (PFP) outlining a **structural adjustment program**, which includes economic goals and strategies for achieving the objectives.

Fair trade has been proposed as an alternative to the international trade model of development. **Fair trade** means that products are made and traded according to standards that protect workers and small businesses in LDCs. Standards for fair trade are set internationally by Fairtrade Labelling Organizations International (FLO). Ten Thousand Villages, which specializes in handicrafts, is the largest fair trade organization in North America. Two sets of standards distinguish fair trade; one set applies to workers on farms and in factories and the other to producers.

The world is clearly divided into regions that have differing levels of economic development. The **core-periphery model** explains this in a simplified way. The wealthiest countries are the core and the less developed countries are on the periphery. There are some countries, like Chile, Brazil, and China that don't easily fit into either and are thus sometimes described as **semi-peripheral.** Immanuel **Wallerstein's World Systems Theory** is similar to the core-periphery model. Wallerstein believed that the concept of core-periphery developed in the fifteenth century as Europeans began to explore and control the globe. His theory describes the world as an interdependent system of countries linked by political and economic competition. **Dependency theory** speaks to continued dependency of LDCs on MDCs where the elite in a developing country will control the vast majority of the wealth and resources of that country.

Key Issues Revisited

9.4. Why do countries face obstacles to development?

- LDCs choose between the international trade and self-sufficiency paths towards development; either way they have to borrow major funds to promote development
- The inability of LDCs to pay back loans causes considerable tension between LDCs and MDCs

Review Questions

9.4.1. At which stage of Rostow's Model would a group of elites introduce innovative economic policies?

A. Stage 5

B. Stage 4

C. Stage 3

D. Stage 2

E. Stage 1

9.4.2. A country that has accumulated 50% or more of debt as a percentage of GDP would be which of the following?

A. the United States

B. Brazil

C. India

D. Spain

E. All of these countries meet the criteria

Key Terms

Core-periphery model
Dependency theory
Developed country
Developing country
Development
Fair trade
Foreign direct investment
Gender Empowerment Measure (GEM)
Gender Inequality Index (GII)
Gross domestic product (GDP)
Human Development Index (HDI)
International Monetary Fund (IMF)
Less developed country (LDC)
Literacy rate
More developed country (MDC)

Nolan's stages of growth model
Primary sector
Productivity
Purchasing Power Parity (PPI)
Rostow's Development Model
Secondary sector
Semi-periphery
Structural adjustment program
Tertiary sector
Transnational Corporation
Value added
Wallerstein's World Systems Theory
World Bank
World Trade Organization (WTO)

Think Like a Geographer Activities

Compare Saudi Arabia's levels of development in terms of gross domestic product, gender inequality, and education. What might account for the discrepancies between these indices?

Quick Quiz

9.1. Development is
A. the process that aids people's intellectual ability.
B. the process used to aid in a factory's output.
C. the process of improving the material conditions of people through technology and knowledge.
D. the process of manufacturing efficiently.
E. the process of giving children in Africa a free laptop.

9.2. All of these are considered developed nations according to the UN **EXCEPT**
A. Canada.
B. Japan.
C. Australia.
D. Russia.
E. United States.

9.3. The United Nations expect that children in developed nations spend the average of
_____ years in school
A. 16
B. 11
C. 12
D. 7
E. 9

9.4. _____ is used to adjust a country's gross national income to account for the cost of
goods in a country.
A. GDP
B. GII
C. PPP
D. GEM
E. IMR

9.5. Which country holds the greatest share of the world's energy demand?
A. Japan
B. Brazil
C. Russia
D. China
E. The United States

Free Response

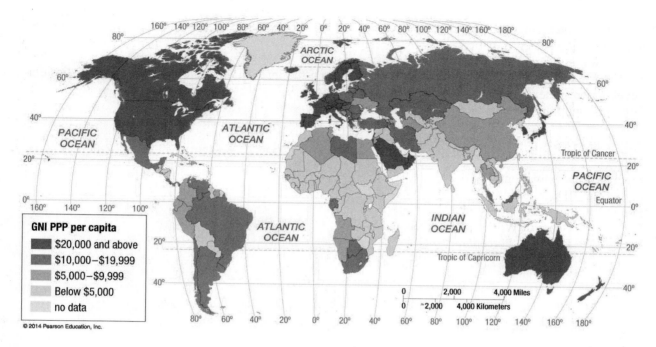

Figure 9-1 Income

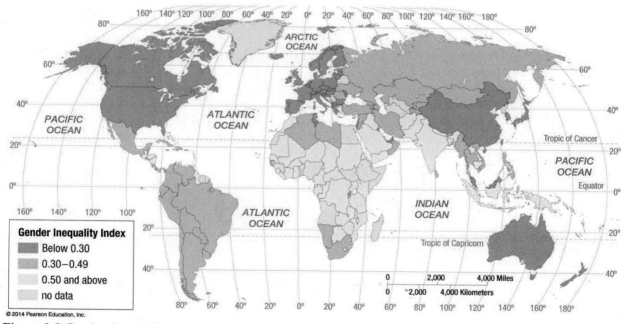

Figure 9-2 Gender Inequality Index

Look at the maps above to answer the following free response question:
A. Identify the regions with the highest income and lowest inequality index.
B. Explain the correlation between income and inequality.
C. Identify one country where this correlation does not hold true.

On the Web

http://www.masteringgeography.com
http://hdr.undp.org/en/statistics/
http://www.cgdev.org/section/initiatives/_active/cdi/
http://www.unesco.org/new/en/education/themes/leading-the-international-agenda/efareport/statistics/efa-development-index/
http://hdr.undp.org/en/statistics/gii/

Key Figures

Figure 9-1 Development Regions
Figure 9-3 HDI by Region
Figure 9-6 Inequality Adjusted HDI
Figure 9-27 Share of World Energy Demand
Figure 9-57 Debt as a Percentage of GNI

Chapter

10 Food and Agriculture

Where Did Agriculture Originate?

This chapter deals with the major primary sector economic activity—agriculture. The origins and diffusion of agriculture are considered first. Farming varies around the world because of a variety of cultural and physical environmental factors. Agriculture is very different in less and more developed regions. In less developed regions, dominated by subsistence agriculture, farm products are usually consumed near to where they are produced. Commercial farming is the norm in more developed countries and farmers sell what they produce. Farmers face numerous problems in each type of region.

> **Learning Outcome 10.1.1:** Identify the major crop and livestock hearths.
>
> Agriculture was invented approximately 10,000 years ago in multiple hearths of crops and livestock.
>
> **Learning Outcome 10.1.2:** Describe the major differences between subsistence and commercial agriculture.
>
> Subsistence agriculture, practiced in developing countries, is characterized by a high percentage of farmers in the labor force, limited use of machinery, and small average farm size. A small percentage of farmers in the labor force, heavy use of machinery, and large average farm size characterize commercial agriculture, practiced in developed countries.

Prior to the invention of agriculture, humans lived as nomadic **hunters and gatherers,** traveling in small groups and collecting food daily. Over thousands of years, plant cultivation evolved through a combination of accident and deliberate experiment. In this way, about 10,000 years ago, people started to practice **agriculture**, the deliberate modification of Earth's surface through the cultivation of plants and

domestication of animals, for sedentary food production. This is known as the **Neolithic (or First) Agricultural Revolution**. The word *cultivate* means "to care for," and a **crop** is any plant cultivated by people.

According to the geographer Carl Sauer, there were two initial types of cultivation. The first was **vegetative planting**, which is the reproduction of plants by direct cloning from existing plants. **Seed agriculture** came later; this is the reproduction of plants of seeds. This is practiced by most farmers today.

There were probably a number of **agricultural hearths** for both vegetative planting and seed agriculture. Sauer believes that vegetative planting originated in South East Asia and diffused from there to other parts of Asia, the Middle East, Africa, and Southern Europe. There may have been other independent vegetative hearths in West Africa and South America.

Sauer identified numerous hearths for seed agriculture, in Asia, Africa, and the Americas. Agriculture and animal domestication had multiple hearths because, to a certain extent, the physical environment determines the food that will be produced.

In **subsistence agriculture**, found in less developed countries (LDCs), farmers produce goods to provide for themselves and others in the local community. **Commercial agriculture**, found in more developed countries (MDCs), is the production of food for competitive, free market sale. This type of agriculture emerged as a result of increased farming technology that was developed during the **Second Agricultural Revolution** in the years preceding the Industrial Revolution in eighteenth century Europe. In **planned agricultural economies**, which are associated with communist countries, the government controls the supply and price of agricultural goods.

Five principal features distinguish commercial from subsistence agriculture. First, as mentioned above, the purpose of farming is different in LDCs and MDCs. Second, agriculture in LDCs is more **labor intensive** rather than the **capital intensive** agriculture which is the norm in MDCs. Thus there will always be a higher percentage of the labor force involved in agriculture in the developing world. Third and related to the percentage of farmers in the labor force, agriculture in developed countries involves more machinery and technology. Fourth, farm size is larger in commercial agriculture, especially in the

United States and Canada. The loss of very productive farmland, known as **prime agricultural land**, is an increasing problem in the United States because of urban sprawl. Finally, in commercial agriculture there is a close relationship between agriculture and other businesses. This is not the case in subsistence agriculture. In developed countries the system of commercial farming is called **agribusiness** because farming is integrated into a large food production industry.

Key Issues Revisited

10.1. Where did agriculture originate?

- Before the development of agriculture, people survived by hunting and gathering

- Agriculture resulted from thousands of years of experiments and accidents

- Current agricultural practices vary between MDCs and LDCs

Review Questions

10.1.1. Why did the world's population begin to grow about 8,000 years ago?

A. medical advances

B. the agricultural revolution

C. industrialization

D. urbanization

E. migration

10.1.2. What country would have the most amount of hectares of farmland per tractor?

A. the United States

B. Chile

C. Egypt

D. France

E. China

KEY ISSUE 2

Why Do People Consume Different Foods?

Learning Outcome 10.2.1: Explain differences between developed and developing countries in food consumption.

Most humans derive most of their dietary energy through cereal grains, especially wheat, rice, and maize. The primary source of protein is meat products in developed countries and grain in developing countries.

Learning Outcome 10.2.2: Explain the global distribution of undernourishment.

The average individual consumes 50 percent more calories than the recommended minimum, but many in sub-Saharan Africa are getting less than the recommended minimum. Worldwide, an estimated 850 million people are undernourished, nearly all of them in developing countries.

People need food to survive, however, the types of foods people eat around the world vary greatly. The diet of people is dependent on the level of development of a country, the physical environment, and also cultural preferences. Grain accounts for 40% of all dietary energy consumption worldwide. The United Nations estimates that approximately one-eighth of the people on Earth do not have **food security** and that 850 million people are undernourished.

In developed nations most people acquire protein through the consumption of meat products (beef, pork, and chicken), whereas in developing nations they get most protein from cereal products. By far, Africa experiences the greatest extent of undernourishment due to the fact that population growth has put a strain on food production.

Key Issues Revisited

10.2. Why do people consume different foods?

- Most people in LDCs are subsistence farmers, growing crops primarily to feed themselves

- Important types of subsistence agriculture include shifting cultivation, pastoral nomadism, and intensive farming

- Regions where subsistence agriculture is practiced are characterized by a large percentage of the labor force engaged in agriculture

Review Questions

10.2.1. The main source of protein in developed countries comes from

A. tofu.

B. soybeans.

C. wheat.

D. maize.

E. meat.

10.2.2. Among developing regions _____ has had the largest decrease in undernourished people.

A. India

B. Pakistan

C. China

D. Mongolia

E. Vietnam

KEY ISSUE 3

Where Is Agriculture Distributed?

Learning Outcome 10.3.1: Identify the 11 major agricultural regions.

The most widely used map of agriculture divides the world into 11 major regions, including 5 in developing countries and 6 in developed countries.

Learning Outcome 10.3.2: Explain how pastoral nomadism works in the drylands of developing regions.

Pastoral nomadism, which is the herding of animals, is the principal form of agriculture adapted to the dry lands of developing countries.

Learning Outcome 10.3.3: Explain how shifting cultivation works in the tropics of developing regions.

Distinctive features of shifting cultivation include the clearing of land through slashing and burning and the use of fields for only a few years.

Learning Outcome 10.3.4: Explain how intensive subsistence farming works in the high population concentrations of developing regions.

The principal crop in the intensive subsistence region is wet rice. Growing rice is an intensive operation that depends primarily on abundant labor.

Learning Outcome 10.3.5: Describe reasons for growing crops other than wet rice in intensive subsistence regions.

In intensive subsistence areas where the climate is unsuitable for rice, hardier crops are grown, such as wheat and barley. Plantation farming is a form of commercial agriculture conducted in developing regions. Plantations grow crops primarily for export to developed countries.

Learning Outcome 10.3.6: Describe how mixed crop and livestock farming works.

Mixed crop and livestock farming is the most common form of agriculture in the center of the United States. Crops, especially maize and soybeans, are grown primarily to feed animals.

Learning Outcome 10.3.7: Describe how dairy farming and commercial gardening work.

Dairy farming is especially important near major population concentrations in developed countries.
Commercial gardening is the predominant form of agriculture in the southeastern United States. These farms specialize in fruits and vegetables preferred by relatively wealthy consumers in developed countries.

Learning Outcome 10.3.8: Describe how grain and Mediterranean farming work.

Grain, especially wheat, is grown in areas that are too dry for mixed crop and livestock farming. Mediterranean agriculture specializes in crops such as grapes and olives.

Learning Outcome 10.3.9: Describe how livestock ranching works.

Livestock is raised on land that is too dry for growing crops.

Shifting cultivation is practiced in much of the world's tropical regions. Farmers clear land for planting by slashing vegetation and burning the debris; this is called **slash and burn agriculture**. The cleared land is called **swidden** and crops grown will include rice (Asia), maize and manioc (South America), millet and sorghum (Africa). Farmers will only grow crops on a cleared field for a few years until the soil nutrients are depleted and then they will leave it **fallow** (nothing planted) so that it can recover. Shifting cultivation occupies about one-fourth of the world's land area but supports less than 5% of the world's population. As rain forests are being cut, shifting cultivation is declining, especially in the Amazon basin. It is being replaced by logging, cattle ranching, and cash crops.

Pastoral nomadism is another type of **extensive subsistence agriculture** that involves nomadic **animal husbandry**. It is practiced in the dry climates of the developing world. The livestock provide food, clothing, and shelter. The animals will vary depending on cultural preferences and physical geography but may include goats, camels, horses, sheep, or cattle. Pastoral nomads have a strong sense of territoriality which determines the land that they occupy. Some pastoral nomads practice **transhumance** which is the seasonal movement of livestock between mountains and lowland pasture areas. **Pasture** is grass or other plants grown for feeding livestock, as well as land used for grazing. This type of agricultural system is on the decline as modern technology is resulting in the conversion of land from nomadic to sedentary agriculture.

Some subsistence agriculture is **intensive** where farmers work land more intensively to subsist. **Intertillage** or field clearance is usually very labor intensive because of a lack of modern machinery. **Intensive subsistence agriculture** is practiced in much of Asia on small plots and mostly by hand. **Wet rice** is the dominant crop in Southeast Asia including China. Wet rice is planted in dry soil in a nursery and then moved to seedlings in a flooded field. The flooded field is called a **sawah (paddy** is the Malay word for wet rice).When the rice is harvested, the husks, known as **chaff,** are separated from the seeds when their heads are **threshed** by being beaten on the ground. When the threshed rice is placed on a tray, the lighter chaff is **winnowed** or blown away by the wind. If the rice is to be consumed by the farmer, the **hull,** or outer covering, is removed by mortar and pestle. In parts of Asia farmers can get two harvests per year from one field. This is known as **double cropping**. Where wet rice is not dominant in Asia, more than one harvest can be obtained each year through **crop rotation**, which is the practice of using different fields from crop to crop each year to avoid soil exhaustion.

Plantation agriculture is the only significant large-scale commercial agriculture in the developing world. Plantations will specialize in crops that will usually be exported to other countries such as sugarcane and coffee. They have typically been owned by foreign companies and are very labor intensive.

Mixed crop and livestock farming is practiced in much of the United States and Northern Europe. Most of the crops are fed to animals. Corn (maize) is generally the crop of choice because of its high yields per area, followed by soybeans.

Dairy farming is an important type of commercial agriculture near urban areas in North America and Europe. The ring surrounding a city from which milk can be supplied without spoiling is called the **milkshed**. Increasingly in the developed world, thanks to modern transportation systems, dairy production can take place further from the market. Dairy farmers are facing economic difficulties because of declining revenues and increasing costs. Other problems inherent to dairy farming include the fact that it is very labor intensive (cows must be milked twice a day), as well as the need for expensive **winter feed**.

Commercial grain farming, which includes wheat and corn, takes place in western North America and southern Russia. In North America there is a **winter wheat** belt in Kansas, Colorado, and Oklahoma where the crop is planted in the autumn. In the **spring wheat** belt, which includes the Dakotas, Montana, and southern Saskatchewan, the crop is planted in the spring. A third important grain growing region is in the state of Washington. Large-scale wheat production was first made possible by the McCormick **reaper** in the 1830s. Today the **combine** performs the three tasks of reaping, threshing, and cleaning in one operation.

Livestock ranching is the extensive commercial grazing of livestock land in semiarid or arid lands. It is practiced in much of the western United States and the pampas regions of Argentina, southern Brazil, and Uruguay. Historically ranching involved the herding of cattle over open ranges in a seminomadic style, and later became sedentary farming by dividing open land into ranches. Today it has become part of the meat-processing industry rather than an economic activity practiced on isolated farms. **Feedlots** are often used for more cost efficient livestock fattening.

Mediterranean agriculture, practiced in the Mediterranean, California, and parts of Chile, Australia, and South Africa, consists of diverse specialty crops such as grapes, olives, nuts, fruits, and vegetables mostly for human consumption. **Horticulture** is the term for the growing of fruits, vegetables, and flowers.

Commercial gardening and fruit farming is the dominant form of agriculture in the Southeastern United States. It is practiced close to urban areas and is also called **truck farming** because "truck" was the Middle English word for barter or the exchange of commodities. Truck farms grow fruits and vegetables.

Key Issues Revisited

10.3. Where is agriculture distributed?

- The most common type of farm found in MDCs is mixed crop and livestock

- Where mixed crop and livestock is not suitable, commercial farmers practice a variety of other types of agriculture, including dairying, commercial grain, and ranching

Review Questions

10.3.1. Intensive subsistence agriculture would be found in

A. East Asia and Southwest Asia.

B. East Asia and South Asia.

C. Latin America and Southeast Asia.

D. Southeast Asia and sub-Saharan Africa

E. South Asia and Latin America.

10.3.2. In which country would you find pastoral nomads?

A. Kazakhstan

B. China

C. Israel

D. Saudi Arabia

E. All of these countries have nomads.

KEY ISSUE 4

Why Do Farmers Face Economic Difficulties?

Learning Outcome 10.4.1: Describe the impact of population growth and trade on farming in developing countries.

Due to rapid population growth, subsistence farmers must feed more people. Pressure to contribute to international trade means that subsistence farmers increasingly grow crops to export rather than to consume at home.

Learning Outcome 10.4.2: Explain the impact of overproduction and market access on farming in developed countries.

Because of their efficiency, commercial farmers produce more food than can be consumed in developed countries.

Learning Outcome 10.4.3: Explain the contribution of expanding exports and farmland to world food supply.

Export of food has increased rapidly, although only a handful of countries produce enough to be major exporters. Historically, agricultural output was increased by expanding the amount of land that is farmed, but expansion of farmland has slowed in recent decades.

Learning Outcome 10.4.4: Describe the contribution of fishing to world food supply.

Fish consumption is increasing but accounts for a small percentage of the average human's diet. Fish production has increased primarily through aquaculture rather than catching of wild fish.

Learning Outcome 10.4.5: Describe the contribution of higher productivity to world food supply.

Agricultural productivity has increased sharply, especially through the invention of higher-yield seeds and expanded use of fertilizers. Despite advances, food prices in the early twenty-first century have been at a record high.

Learning Outcome 10.4.6: Describe the role of sustainable agriculture in world food supply.

Sustainable agriculture involves sensitive land management, limited use of chemicals, and better integration of crops and livestock. Sustainable agriculture accounts for a small but increasing share of world agriculture.

The **von Thunen model** helps to explain the importance of proximity to market and the choice of crops in commercial agriculture. Johann von Thunen published his model in a book titled *The Isolated*

State in 1826. According to von Thunen, rent, or land value, will decrease the further one gets from a market. Thus the agricultural products that use the land most intensively, have the highest transportation costs, are more perishable, and are in the greatest demand, such as dairying and fruits and vegetables, will be located close to the market. Agriculture that uses the land more extensively, such as livestock ranching, will be further away from the market.

Von Thunen placed horticulture and dairying closest to the city, followed by forestry (for fuel and building). The next rings were used for various crops and pasture becoming more extensive further from the market. The model had various assumptions that may not have been true in reality, such as a uniform landscape, equal ease of transportation in all directions, and a single market.

Although *The Isolated State* is a dated and oversimplified model of reality, the principles of agricultural location still apply today especially at a national or global scale, and it still describes the actual patterns of land use surrounding many cities.

Agricultural regions are largely determined by climate and, to a lesser extent cultural preferences. In addition there are two important economic considerations for subsistence farmers. These include rapid population growth and the demands of the international market.

According to Esther Boserup as population has increased in subsistence economies, farmers have intensified production by leaving land fallow for shorter periods and by the adoption of new farming methods.

In some LDCs such as Kenya, families may divide by gender between traditional subsistence agriculture and the growing of crops for export. Women practice most of the subsistence agriculture while men grow crops for export, one of the legacies of colonial agricultural systems, or work in urban jobs. The export crops grown in some LDCs, especially in Latin America and Asia, are those that can be converted to drugs.

Sub-Saharan African countries have been encouraged by the United States to increase their food supply in part by increased use of **biotechnology** or **genetic modification (GM)** of crops and livestock which could increase yields, nutrition, and provide more resistance to pests.

Overproduction is a problem in commercial farming, especially the United States and Europe. Even though demand has remained constant, the U.S. government has tried to alleviate the problem by developing three policies. Farmers are encouraged to avoid producing crops that are in excess supply. The government will pay farmers when certain prices are low, and they will buy surplus production and sell or donate it to foreign governments.

Sustainable agriculture is becoming more widespread in MDCs. This type of agriculture promotes environmental quality through sensitive land management, limited use of chemicals, and integrating the growing of crops and raising of livestock. One type of land management is **ridge tillage** which is the planting of crops on ridge tops to conserve soil.

Food supply can be increased in the world by initiating a number of strategies. Expansion of land under production is one method, although this can lead to environmental problems such as **desertification** in arid regions. Soil salinity has also been a problem where irrigated agriculture is practiced in hot, arid regions. The **Green Revolution** (also known as the **Third Agricultural Revolution)** which involved the use of new higher-yield seeds as well as fertilizers during the 1970s and 1980s has resulted in increased food supply in parts of Asia and Latin America. Strategies are now being developed to expand **aquaculture**, fish farming or the cultivation of the oceans. Higher-protein cereals are being developed in MDCs, and the palatability of rarely consumed foods, like soybean, is being improved. Another alternative for increasing the world's food supply is to export more food from MDCs that produce surpluses to LDCs, especially in Africa that are experiencing a food-supply crisis.

Key Issues Revisited

10.4. Why do farmers face economic difficulties?

- Problems with agriculture in LDCs are associated with rapid population growth and pressure to adopt international trade strategies to promote development

- Problems with agriculture in MDCs result from access to markets and overproduction

Review Questions

10.4.1. About 90% of the world's opium comes from

A. Myanmar.

B. Colombia.

C. Mexico.

D. Afghanistan.

E. Europe.

10.4.2. The largest yields of fishing come from

A. the Pacific and Asia.

B. the Atlantic Northeast and inland Europe.

C. the Atlantic Northeast and Asia.

D. the Pacific and inland Europe.

E. the Atlantic Northeast and Eastern Indian Ocean.

Key Terms

Agribusiness
Agriculture
Agricultural hearths
Animal husbandry
Aquaculture
Biotechnology
Capital-intensive
Cereal grain
Chaff
Combine
Commercial agriculture
Commercial gardening and fruit farming
Commercial grain farming
Crop
Crop rotation
Dairy farming
Desertification
Domestication
Double cropping
Extensive subsistence agriculture
Fallow
Feedlots
Genetic modification (GM)
Grain
Green Revolution
Horticulture
Hull
Hunters and gatherers
Intensive subsistence agriculture
Intertillage
Labor-intensive
Livestock ranching

Mediterranean agriculture
Milkshed
Mixed crop and livestock farming Neolithic Agricultural Revolution
Paddy
Pastoral nomadism
Pasture
Planned agricultural economies
Plantation
Prime agricultural land
Ranching
Reaper
Ridge tiller
Sawah
Second Agricultural Revolution
Seed agriculture
Slash-and-burn agriculture
Shifting cultivation
Spring wheat
Subsistence agriculture
Sustainable agriculture
Swidden
Third Agricultural Revolution
Thresh
Transhumance
Truck farming
Vegetative planting
Von Thunen Model
Wet rice
Winnow
Winter feed
Winter wheat

Think Like a Geographer

Read the following article on the Colombian Exchange:
http://pubs.aeaweb.org/doi/pdfplus/10.1257/jep.24.2.163
Now, draw a sketch map of the world and map the exchanges that are mentioned.

Quick Quiz

10.1. Contemporary hunter and gatherers can be found in all of the following EXCEPT
A. the Great Victoria Desert.
B.   the Rhone Valley.
C. India's Andaman Islands.
D. Botswana.
E. Namibia.

10.2. A hearth for beans and corn is
A. Peru.
B. Brazil.
C. Mexico.
D. Guatemala.
E. Venezuela.

10.3. Diffusion of the domesticated horse most certainly is associated with
A. the diffusion of food preferences to eat horsemeat.
B. the diffusion of corn.
C. the diffusion of the potato.
D. the diffusion of the Indo-European language.
E. the diffusion of the Sino-Tibetan language.

10.4. The main features that distinguish commercial and subsistence agriculture include
A. a small percentage of farmers engaged in agriculture.
B. a small agricultural density.
C. the dependence on machinery.
D. a large farm size.
E. All of these features are relevant to commercial agriculture.

10.5. The type of commercial agriculture found in developing countries is
A. plantation farming.
B. mixed crop and livestock.
C. dairy farming.
D. grain farming.
E. commercial gardening.

10.6. All of these are strategies to increase the world's food supply EXCEPT
A. increase exports from countries with surpluses.
B. expand the land area used for agriculture.
C. create government policy that place people on strict diets.
D. increase agriculture land production.
E. expand fishing.

Free Response

A. Describe and explain why commercial farmers suffer from low incomes in developed countries.
B. List and explain strategies that governments in developed countries implement in order to help address the aforementioned problem.

On the Web

http://www.masteringgeography.com
http://www.mapsofworld.com/thematic-maps/world-food-consumption-map.htm
http://www.time.com/time/photogallery/0,29307,1626519,00.html
http://www.differencebetween.com/difference-between-subsistence-farming-and-vs-commercial-farming/
http://www.bbc.co.uk/schools/gcsebitesize/geography/rural_environments/farming_rural_areas_rev1.shtml
http://www.wfp.org/hunger/malnutrition
http://www.cbd.int/agro/whatstheproblem.shtml

Key Figures

Figure 10-4 Animal Hearths
Figure 10-14 Income Spent on Food
Figure 10-15 Distribution of Undernourishment
Figure 10-44 Meat Production
Figure 10-60 Major Fishing Regions

Chapter

11 Industry and Manufacturing

Where Is Industry Distributed?

This chapter outlines the regions where industry is located and why. The two most important considerations regarding location are where the markets for the products are located and where the necessary resources are located. Increasingly industry has diffused from MDCs to LDCs, especially through the operation of transnational corporations.

Learning Outcome 11.1.1: Describe the locations of the principal industrial regions.

Most of the world's industry is clustered in the three regions: Europe, North America, and East Asia.

The **Industrial Revolution** originated in Britain during the late eighteenth century because of the combination of entrepreneurs, capital, raw materials, and available labor. It also included social and political changes but it generally refers to the economic changes that began in Britain in the late 1700s. Prior to the Industrial Revolution small-scale manufacturing was home-based and known as the **cottage industry.** The Industrial Revolution resulted in major changes for the iron and steel industry, coal mining, transportation, textiles, chemicals, and food processing.

Each of the following three regions accounts for roughly one-fourth of the world's total industrial output: Europe, North America, and East Asia. The other leading industrial producers are Brazil and India.

Western Europe has major industrialization regions in Britain, the Rhine-Ruhr Valley, the mid-Rhine, and northern Italy. Britain's is the oldest of these industrial regions, and with the decline of traditional industry it was able to attract high-tech industries in the late twentieth century, especially Japanese companies. The Rhine-Ruhr has been important largely because of coal and iron deposits, and steel making. The mid-Rhine includes parts of Germany and France, and has been important because of its proximity to large consumer markets. The Po valley of northern Italy began with **textile** manufacturing and has benefited from low labor costs. Northeastern Spain was Western Europe's fastest growing industrial area in the late twentieth century, especially in the motor-vehicle industry.

The oldest industrial areas in Eastern Europe are the central industrial district, which is centered on Moscow, and the St. Petersburg industrial district which was one of Russia's early nodes of industrial development. Other industrial areas in Eastern Europe include the Volga industrial district, particularly important for petroleum and natural gas, and the Ural industrial district, which has become a main source of raw materials but lacks energy sources. The Kuznetsk is Russia's most important industrial region east of the Ural Mountains. Outside the former Soviet Union there are important industrial regions in Donetsk, Eastern Ukraine, and Silesia which includes parts of Poland and the Czech Republic.

North America became a major industrial region later than Europe. Textiles were important in the United States by 1860. Manufacturing has been traditionally located in the northeastern United States with its numerous raw materials. These areas include New England, the Middle Atlantic, the Mohawk Valley, and the Pittsburgh-Lake Erie region. The western Great Lakes have also become important, especially because of the dominance of Chicago as a market center. Southern California is the leading U.S. industrial area outside of the Northeast. Canada's most important industrial area is in southeastern Ontario, benefiting from its location and the availability of cheap hydroelectric power.

East Asia has become a major industrial region since the second half of the twentieth century by taking advantage of its large labor force. Japan emerged first, followed by South Korea, Taiwan, and China. The latter is now the world's largest manufacturer of textiles and apparel, steel, and many household products. It also has the world's largest supply of low-cost labor and the world's largest market for many consumer products.

Key Issues Revisited

11.1. Where is industry distributed?

- Industry has been concentrated in three regions during the twentieth century: Europe, North America, and East Asia

Review Questions

11.1.1. One of the major catalysts for the industrial revolution in England was

A. Adam Smith's *Wealth of a Nation.*

B. James Watt's steam engine.

C. Henry Ford's assembly line.

D. Horace Greeley's "manifest destiny."

E. Steve Job's microprocessor.

11.1.2. Canada's most important industrial area is

A. Southeastern Ontario.

B. the Mohawk Valley.

C. the St. Lawrence Seaway.

D. the western Great Lakes.

E. the Prairie Provinces.

KEY ISSUE 2

Why Are Situation and Site Factors Important?

Learning Outcome 11.2.1: Explain the two types of situation factors and why some industries locate near inputs.

Situation factors involve minimizing the cost of shipping from sources of inputs or to markets. A location near sources of inputs is optimal for bulk-reducing industries. Industries that extract a large amount of minerals tend to be bulk-reducing industries.

Learning Outcome 11.2.1: Explain why some industries locate near markets.

Bulk-gaining industries, single-market manufacturers, and perishable products companies tend to locate near markets.

Learning Outcome 11.2.3: Explain why industries use different types of transportation.

Trucks are most often used for short-distance delivery, trains for longer trips within a region, ships for ocean crossings, and planes for very high-value packages. Some firms locate near break-of-bulk points, where goods are transferred between modes of transportation.

Learning Outcome 11.2.4: Explain how the optimal location for steel production has changed.

Steel production has traditionally been located near inputs, but the relative importance of the two main inputs—coal and iron ore—has changed. Some steel production, especially mini-mills, is now located near the markets. Industries that extract a large amount of minerals tend to be bulk-reducing industries.

Learning Outcome 11.2.5: Explain the distribution of motor vehicle production.

Because they are bulk-gaining products, most motor vehicles are assembled near their markets. The distribution of motor vehicle production has changed because the distribution of buyers has changed.

Learning Outcome 11.2.6: Explain the three types of site factors.

The three site factors are labor, capital, and land. A labor-intensive industry has a high percentage of labor in the production process.

Learning Outcome 11.2.7: Explain the distribution of textile and apparel production.

The clothing industry is a labor-intensive industry. Three steps in production are spinning, weaving, and sewing. Most spinning and weaving occur in low-wage countries, but some sewing occurs in developed countries near consumers.

Situation factors involve decisions about industrial location that attempt to minimize transportation costs by considering raw material source(s) as well as the market(s). If the cost of transporting the inputs is greater than the cost of transporting the finished product, the best plant location is nearer to the inputs. Otherwise the best location for the factory will be closer to the consumers.

The North American copper industry is a good example of locating near the raw material source. Copper concentration is a **bulk-reducing industry**; the final product weighs less than the inputs. Two-thirds of U.S. copper is mined in Arizona so most of the concentration mills and smelters are also in Arizona. Steelmaking is another bulk-reducing industry. Steel was made by the Bessemer process, invented in 1855, which combined iron ore and carbon at very high temperatures using coal to produce steel. By the beginning of the twentieth century most large U.S. steel mills were located near the East and West coasts because iron ore was coming from other countries.

Today the U.S steel industry is located near major markets in minimills. It has become a **footloose industry**, which can locate virtually anywhere because the main input is scrap metal and is available almost everywhere. Today the U.S. steel industry takes advantage of **agglomeration economies**, or sharing of services with other companies that are available at major markets. The agglomeration of companies can lead to the development of **ancillary activities** that surround and support large-scale industry. This will result in continued growth which is called **cumulative causation. Deglomeration** occurs when a firm leaves an agglomerated region to start in a distant, new place. However, according to Alfred Weber's theory of industrial location or **least-cost theory**, firms will locate where they can minimize transportation and labor costs as well as take advantage of agglomeration economies.

The location of **bulk-gaining industries** is determined largely by the markets because they gain volume or weight during production. Most drink bottling industries are examples of bulk-gaining industries; empty cans or bottles are brought to the bottler, filled and shipped to consumers.

Single-market manufacturers are specialized, with only one or two customers, such as manufacturers of motor vehicle parts. Obviously they will tend to cluster around their customers. Perishable-product industries such as fresh food and newspapers will usually locate near their markets.

Transportation costs will decline with distance because loading and unloading costs are the greatest. The major modes of transportation are ship, rail, truck, and air. A **break-of-bulk point** is a place transfer from one mode of transportation to another is possible.

Site factors include labor, land, and capital. **Labor-intensive industries** are those where the highest percentage of expenses are the cost of employees, such as textile and apparel production. Land, which includes natural resources, is a major site factor. City sites offer proximity to a large supply of labor as well as to sources of capital. More recently factories are locating in suburban and rural locations because land is cheaper and proximity to highways is more important now. There are also important environmental factors. For example, aluminum producers locate near dams to take advantage of hydroelectric power. The availability of capital is critical to the location of high-tech industries such as those in California's Silicon Valley. The distribution of industries in LDCs is largely dependent on the ability to borrow money.

Key Issues Revisited

11.2. Why are situation and site factors important?

- Factories try to identify a location where location costs are minimized

- Critical industrial location costs include situation factors for some firms and site factors for others

- Situation factors involve the cost of transporting both inputs into the factory and products from the factory to the consumer

- Three site factors—land, labor, and capital—control the cost of doing business at a location

Review Questions

11.2.1. Few important minerals would be found in

A. Europe.

B. Central Asia.

C. Southwest Asia.

D. Northern Africa.

E. All of these regions lack important minerals.

11.2.2. The world's largest steel producing nation in 2010 was

A. Russia.

B. the United States.

C. Japan.

D. England.

E. China.

KEY ISSUE 3

Where Does Industry Cause Pollution?

Learning Outcome 11.3.1: Explain reasons for global warming and damage to the ozone layer.

Air pollution occurs at global, regional, and local scales. At the global scale, the principal pollution is global warming, caused primarily by burning of fossil fuels in factories and vehicles.

Learning Outcome 11.3.2: Explain regional and local-scale air pollution and solid waste pollution.

Acid deposition is a major form of regional-scale air pollution. Sulfuric acid and nitric acid generated by burning of fossil fuels fall into bodies of water. Carbon monoxide, hydrocarbons, and particulates are the major forms of local-scale air pollution. Solid waste is typically placed in landfills or incinerated.

Learning Outcome 11.3.3: Explain differences between point and nonpoint sources of water pollution.

Point-source pollution originates from a specific place, such as a pipe, generated principally by factories and sewage disposal. Nonpoint sources are generated primarily by agricultural runoff.

Air, water, and land remove and disperse waste, but **pollution** will occur when more waste is added than a resource can accommodate. **Air pollution** is a concentration of trace substances at a greater level than occurs in average air. The burning of fossil fuels generates most air pollution. Air pollution may contribute to global warming because of the **greenhouse effect**, which is when carbon dioxide traps some of the radiation emitted by Earth's surface. The **ozone** layer of Earth's atmosphere absorbs dangerous ultra violet (UV) rays from the Sun but is threatened by pollutants called **chlorofluorocarbons (CFCs)**.

Pollution in the form of tiny droplets of sulfuric acid and nitric acid, formed as a result of the emission of burning fossil fuels, return to Earth's surface as **acid deposition**. When dissolved in water, the acids may fall as **acid precipitation, which** damages lakes and agricultural land in regions of heavy industrial development. Urban air pollution consists of carbon monoxide, hydrocarbons, and particulates. In the presence of sunlight this forms **photochemical smog, which** is a serious problem in many urban areas.

Most water pollution is generated by water-using industries, municipal sewage, and agriculture. Polluted water can harm aquatic plants and animals. It also causes waterborne diseases such as cholera, typhoid, and dysentery, especially in LDCs that suffer from poor sanitation and untreated water. It also harms aquatic plants and animals as the water becomes oxygen starved and fish die (**biochemical oxygen demand**).

Paper products constitute the largest percentage of solid waste in the United States. Most of this waste is disposed in **sanitary landfills**. The number of landfills in the United States has declined by three-fourths since 1990; there are now a smaller number of larger regional landfills. Incineration reduces the bulk of trash by about three-fourths, but burning releases toxins into the air. The disposal of hazardous waste is especially difficult. Hazardous waste sites, such as Love Canal, near Niagara Falls, New York, have leaked and caused health problems.

Key Issues Revisited

11.3. Why does industry cause pollution?

- Industry is a major polluter of air, water and land

- Pollution occurs when more waste is added than Earth is capable of handling

- The world's richest countries tend to be the greatest polluters

Review Questions

11.3.1. The worst air pollution in the United States would be found in

A. New York, NY.

B. Denver, CO.

C. Los Angeles, CA.

D. Seattle, WA.

E. St. Louis, MO.

11.3.2. The largest polluters of toxic waste are

A. nuclear power plants.

B. coal burning plants.

C. wind farms.

D. mines.

E. research labs.

KEY ISSUE 4

Why are Situation and Site Factors Changing?

Learning Outcome 11.4.1: Explain reasons for changing distribution of industry within the United States.

Industry is moving from the North to the South within the United States. Lower labor costs and absence of unions are major factors in the migration.

Learning Outcome 11.4.2: Explain reasons for the emergence of new industrial regions.

Some jobs have been transferred to low-wage countries as part of the new international division of labor. The BRIC countries (Brazil, Russia, India, and China) are expected to be the top industrial powers by the middle of the twenty-first century.

Learning Outcome 11.4.3: Explain reasons for renewed attraction of traditional industrial regions.

Traditional industrial regions attract and retain industries that need skilled labor. Just-in-time delivery has increased the attraction of locating near consumers.

Within regions in MDCs industry has relocated to urban peripheries and rural areas from central city locations. At the interregional level manufacturing has moved towards the south and west in the United States. Historically industrial growth has been encouraged in the South by government policies to reduce regional disparities. Southern states have enacted **right-to-work laws** that require factories to maintain an "open shop" and prohibit a "closed shop." In a closed shop everyone who works in the factory has to join the union. Thus Southern right-to-work laws have made it much more difficult for unions to organize, collect dues, and bargain. States that have passed these laws are called **right-to-work states.**

In Western Europe government policies and those of the European Union have also encouraged industry to move from traditional industrial centers in northwestern Europe toward southern and Eastern Europe. For example Spain's textile and motor-vehicle manufacturing industries have grown substantially since its admission to the European Union in 1986.

Some central European countries such as Poland, the Czech Republic, and Hungary have received industrial investment since the fall of communism in the early 1990s. They offer less skilled but cheaper labor than Western Europe and have locations that are close to major markets.

In 1970 nearly one-half of world industry was in Europe and nearly one-third was in North America; now these two regions account for only one-fourth each. The share of world industry in other regions has increased from one-sixth in 1970 to one-half in 2010. These regions include East Asia, South Asia, and Latin America.

As industry has declined in MDCs, it has increased in LDCs. In 1980 80% of the world's steel was produced in MDCs. Between 1980 and 2008, MDC's share of steel production declined to 40%, and that of LDCs increased to 60%.

China is the leading new industrial center in the world because of its low labor costs and vast consumer market. Mexico and Brazil are the leading industrial centers in Latin America, with manufacturing clustered near large cities such as Mexico City and Sao Paulo. Since the 1980s manufacturing in Mexico has moved north to take advantage of the U.S. market, and **maquiladora** plants have been established close to the U.S. border. Maquiladoras, which assemble U.S. parts and ship the finished product back to the United States, have benefited from the **North American Free Trade Agreement (NAFTA).** NAFTA has eliminated restrictions on the flow of materials and products between the United States and Mexico.

The cost of labor is changing the spatial organization of industry around the world. This is particularly true of the textile and apparel industry. In the twentieth century production in the United States moved from the Northeast to the Southeast to take advantage of cheaper wages. More recently the apparel industry is located in Latin America, China, and other Asian countries. Now the United States imports more than 75% of its clothing needs. This is one part of the **new international division of labor**. Industrial jobs are transferring to LDCs largely as a result of transnational corporations' search for low-cost labor. **Transnational corporations** are **outsourcing**, turning over much of the responsibility for production to independent suppliers. There is concern that some of these clothes are made in factories called

sweatshops, not unlike those in the early Industrial Revolution, where the working conditions are terrible.

In some MDCs industry is remaining in traditional regions because of skilled labor and rapid delivery to market. The **Fordist** approach, named for Henry Ford, traditionally assigned each worker a specific task in mass production industry. **Post-Fordist** production has recently become the norm in MDCs. It is flexible production with skilled workers characterized by teams working together, problem solving through consensus, and factory workers being treated alike regardless of their level.

Just-in-time delivery is the shipment of parts and materials to a factory immediately before they are needs. It avoids the stocking of unnecessary and expensive inventory. Two kinds of disruption can result from reliance on just-in-time delivery: labor unrest and "Acts of God" (such as a blizzard or flood).

Key Issues Revisited

11.4. Why are situation and site factors changing?

- New industrial regions are able to attract some industries, especially because of low wage rates

- Traditional industrial regions have been able to offer manufacturers skilled workers and proximity to customers demanding just-in-time delivery

Review Questions

11.4.1. One of the main reasons that industry in the United States has shifted its production is

A. that they have moved to states with "closed shops."

B. that they have moved to be closer to illegal laborers.

C. that they have moved to "right to work states."

D. that they have moved for better climate.

E. that they have moved to be closer to iron ore deposits.

11.4.2. According to Goldman Sachs all of these countries are expected to dominate global manufacturing in the twenty-first century EXCEPT

A. the United States.

B. Brazil.

C. China.

D. India.

E. Russia.

Key Terms

Acid deposition
Acid precipitation
Agglomeration economies
Ancillary activities
Biochemical oxygen demand (BOD)
Break-of-bulk point
Bulk-gaining industry
Bulk-reducing industry
Carbon monoxide
Chlorofluorocarbons (CFCs)
Cottage industry
Cumulative causation
Deglomeration
Footloose industry
Fordist
Global warming
Greenhouse effect
Hydrocarbons
Industrial Revolution

Just-in-time delivery
Labor-intensive industry
Least-cost theory
Maquiladora
New international division of labor
North American Free Trade Agreement (NAFTA)
Outsourcing
Particulates
Photochemical smog
Point -source pollution
Post-Fordist
Right-to-work laws
Right-to-work states
Sanitary landfill
Site factors
Situation factors
Sweatshops
Textile
Transnational corporation

Think Like a Geographer Activities

Read the case study on page 413 about Climate Change in the South Pacific, then investigate other parts of the world that seem to be affected by rising temperatures.

Quick Quiz

11.1. Where are almost all of the rare earth metals located?
A. Brazil
B. China
C. Mexico
D. Angola
E. the United States

11.2. The world's three principal industrial regions are
A. Europe, North America, and East Asia.
B. Europe, East Asia, and South Asia.
C. Europe, North America ,and Japan.
D. Europe, North America, and Oceania.
E. Europe, Oceania, and East Asia.

11.3. Why are just-in-time products important for industries?
A. They can be stock piled and used just in the nick of time.
B. They are not perishable so they may be used anytime.
C. They are delivered to the factory right when they are going to be used.
D. They are put on container ships because there is not hurry in the time they will be used.
E. They are used in cottage industries at any time they are needed.

11.4. Who was responsible for patenting an efficient way for casting steel?
A. James Watt
B. Henry Bessemer
C. Nicolas Appert
D. John Roebuck
E. Richard Arkwright

11.5. Why would an industry choose to locate in a traditional region, like the northeastern United States?
A. availability of cheap labor and transportation
B. availability of cheap land and unskilled labor
C. availability of skilled labor and the ability to deliver to the market
D. availability of cheap land and the ability to deliver to the market
E. availability of cheap labor and the ability to deliver to the market

Free Response

Define containerization and break-of-bulk point.
Describe how containerization and break-of-bulk point assist industries in reducing their costs.

On the Web

http://www.masteringgeography.com
http://www.businessdictionary.com/definition/industrial-sector.html
http://www.victorianweb.org/technology/ir/irchron.html
http://www.eh-resources.org/timeline/timeline_industrial.html
http://www.wisegeek.org/what-is-outsourcing.htm
http://ed.ted.com/lessons/how-containerization-shaped-the-modern-world

Key Figures

Figure 11-2 Diffusion of the Industrial Revolution
Figure 11-3 Europe's Industrial Areas
Figure 11-4 North America's Industrial Areas
Figure 11-7 Distribution of Minerals
Figure 11-19 Share of Global Steel Production 1980 and 2010
Figure 11-42 Toxic Chemical Release Sites
Figure 11-46 Changing U.S. Manufacturing

Chapter

12 Services and Settlements

Where Are Services Distributed?

In MDCs most workers are employed in the tertiary sector of the economy, which is the provision of goods and services. There is a close relationship between services and settlements; most services are clustered in settlements. They are also clustered in MDCs because that is where people are more likely to be able to buy services, rather than LDCs. Within MDCs business services locate in large settlements which are also the key markets.

Learning Outcome 12.1.1: Describe the three types of services and changing numbers of types of jobs.

Three types of services are consumer, business, and public. Jobs are growing in the service sector rather than in agriculture and industry.

In North America, three-quarters of employees work in the service sector. There are three types of services: consumer services, business services, and public services.

Consumer services provide services to individual consumers and include retail services and personal services. Retail and wholesale services include about 15% of all jobs in the United States and provide goods for sale to consumers. Other consumer services include education services, health services, and leisure and hospitality services.

Business services help other businesses and include financial services, professional services, transportation and information services; they diffuse and distribute services.

Public services which include governmental services at various levels provide security and protection for citizens and businesses.

All the growth in employment in the United States between 1972 and 2010 has been in the service sector, as employment in primary and secondary sector activities has declined. Within business services, jobs expanded most rapidly in professional services. The most rapid increase within consumer services has been in the provision of health care. There have been other large increases in education, entertainment, and recreation.

Settlements probably originated to provide consumer and public services. Business services came later.

There have been major urban settlements in different parts of the world since ancient times, including Mesopotamia, Greece, and Rome. In ancient Greece **city-states** such as Athens and Sparta,emerged. These included the city and surrounding countryside or hinterland. Athens made major contributions to the development of culture, philosophy, and other elements of Western civilization. This shows that urban settlements have been distinguished from rural ones not only by public services but also by a concentration of consumer services, especially cultural activities. Cities in the Roman world, especially Rome, were important centers of administration, trade, culture, and a host of other services.

Key Issues Revisited

12.1. Where are services distributed?

- Consumer (including retail, health, education, and leisure), business (including financial, professional, and management), and public (including federal, state, and local) are the three types of services

- Services originated in rural settlements, and the earliest services were primarily personal and public

Review Questions

12.1.1. In developing nations less than _____ of the people work in service industries

A. 50%

B. 25%

C. 75%

D. 10%

E. more than 75%

12.1.2. What part of the consumer service industry has not seen an increase in the number of jobs?

A. education

B. health care

C. government

D. retail

E. entertainment

KEY ISSUE 2

Where Are Consumer Services Distributed?

Learning Outcome 12.2.1: Explain the concepts of market area, range, and threshold.

The market area is the area surrounding a service from which customers are attracted. The range is the maximum distance people are willing to travel to use a service. The threshold is the minimum number of people needed to support a service.

Learning Outcome 12.2.2: Explain the distribution of different sized settlements

Larger settlements provide consumer services that have larger thresholds, ranges, and market areas. In many developed countries, settlements follow a regular hierarchy.

Learning Outcome 12.2.3: Explain how to use threshold and range to find the optimal location for a service.

The gravity model predicts that the optimal location of a service is directly related to the number of people in the area and inversely related to the distance people must travel to access it.

Consumer services are generally provided in a regular pattern based on size of settlements, with larger settlements offering more than smaller ones.

Central place theory provides a framework for looking at the relationship between settlements of different sizes, especially their ability to provide various goods and services. It was developed by Walter Christaller in the 1930s, and was based on his studies of settlement patterns in southern Germany. A service will have a **market area** or **hinterland** of potential customers. Each urban settlement will have a market area, assuming that people will get services from the nearest settlement. The **range** is the maximum distance that people are willing to travel for a service, and the **threshold** is the minimum number of people needed to support a service. Retailers and other service providers will use these concepts to analyze the potential market-area. Determining the profitability of a location and optimal location within a market is called **market-area analysis**. Services and settlements are hierarchical, and larger settlements will provide consumer services that have larger thresholds, ranges, and market areas than smaller settlements. Central place theory shows market areas in MDCs as a series of hexagons of various sizes. Christaller identifies four different levels of market area and seven different settlement sizes. Since this is a theory, he made certain assumptions that may or may not be true in reality, such as equal ease of transportation in all directions, and that people would always get a service from the nearest available market.

The **gravity model** predicts that the best location for a service is directly related to the number of people in the area and inversely related to the distance that people must travel for it. A place with more people will have more potential customers, and people who are further away from a service are less likely to use it.

Geographers have observed that, in many MDCs, there is sometimes a regular hierarchy of settlements from largest to smallest. This is the **rank size rule**, where a country's nth-largest settlement is $1/n$th the population of the largest settlement. So the second largest city would be half the size of the largest. The hierarchy of towns and cities in the United States follows the rank size rule fairly well, which shows that goods and services are provided to consumers at many levels throughout the country. Many LDCs as well as some European countries follow the **primate city rule** rather than the rank size rule. A

primate city is much larger and more important than any other city in that country. This is true of Buenos Aires, Argentina, and Copenhagen, Denmark.

In settlements at the lower end of the central place hierarchy, **periodic markets** may be set up. These are collections of individual vendors who offer goods and services in a specific location one of two times a week. They exist all over the globe.

Key Issues Revisited

12.2. Where are consumer services distributed?

- Services are clustered in settlements

- Rural centers are centers for agriculture and provide a small number of services

- Urbanization involves increases in the percentage of and the number of people living in urban settlements

- Urban settlements are centers for consumer and business services

Review Questions

12.2.1. A market area is a good example of a

A. vernacular region.

B. formal region.

C. hierarchical region.

D. functional region.

E. sphere of influence.

12.2.2. When plotted on a logarithmetic paper, states whose cities follow the rank size rule will show cities in a

A. hexagonal shape.

B. circular shape.

C. square shape.

D. triangular shape.

E. straight line.

KEY ISSUE 3

Where Are Business Services Distributed?

Learning Outcome 12.3.1: Describe the four levels of settlements, based on their business services.

Global cities (or world cities) are the centers of the global flows of information and capital.
Below global cities are three other tiers of urban settlements, offering varying types of business services.

Learning Outcome 12.3.2: Explain the two types of business services in developing countries.

Some small countries offer offshore financial services, which attract investors because of low taxes and extreme privacy. Developing countries also specialize in back-office operations, also called business-processing outsourcing.

Learning Outcome 12.3.3: Explain the concept of economic base.

Basic industries export primarily to consumers outside the settlement; they are the principal source of growth and wealth for a settlement. Some settlements attract a disproportionate share of talented individuals.

Modern world cities offer business services especially financial services. They also have retail services with huge market areas, such as leisure and cultural services of national importance. London presents more plays than the rest of Britain combined. World cities are also centers of national and international power. New York is the headquarters of the United Nations, and Brussels is one of the headquarters cities of the European Union.

Geographers have identified four levels of cities. These are global or world cities, command and control centers, specialized producer-service centers, and dependent centers. London, New York, and Tokyo are at the top of the hierarchy of world cities and are considered Alpha ++ cities because they provide many services in the global economy. Global cities are divided according to their economic, political, cultural, and infrastructural factors using the levels alpha, beta, and gamma. There are also second and third tier world cities. Some major corporations and banks have their headquarters in second tier or major world cities. Third tier world cities are called secondary world cities.

Command and control centers contain the headquarters of large corporations, and concentrations of a variety of business services. There are regional centers like Atlanta and Boston, and subregional centers such as Charlotte and Des Moines.

Specialized producer-service centers have management, and research and development activities associated with specific industries. Detroit is a specialized producer-service center specializing in motor vehicles.

As the term suggests, dependent centers depend on decisions made in world cities for their economic wellbeing. They provide relatively unskilled jobs. San Diego is an industrial and military dependent center.

In the global economy, LDCs specialize in two distinctive types of business services—**offshore financial services** and **back-office functions.** Small countries, often islands and microstates, offer offshore financial services. These offshore centers provide tax havens for companies and privacy from disclosure. Back-office functions include processing insurance claims, payroll management, transcription work, and other routine clerical work. Some LDCs have attracted back offices because of low wages and the ability to speak English.

Basic industries are exported mainly to consumers outside a settlement and constitute that community's **economic base.** These industries employ a large percentage of a community's workforce. **Nonbasic industries** are usually consumed within that community. The growth of a community's economy that results from its basic and nonbasic industries is called the **multiplier effect**. Basic industries are vital to the economic health of a settlement. The concept of basic industries originally referred to the secondary sector of the economy, such as manufacturing but in a **postindustrial society** such as the United States, they are now more likely to be in the service sector of the economy.

Key Issue Revisited

12.3. Where are business services distributed?

- Consumer services attract customers from market areas of varying size

- Geographers calculate whether a service can be profitable within a market area

- In MDCs, market areas form a relatively regular hierarchy by size and distance from each other

Review Questions

12.3.1. Global cities typically offer

A. nightclubs.

B. theaters.

C. libraries.

D. sporting events.

E. all of these.

12.3.2. An example of a back-office function would be

A. performing dental work.

B. performing orthopedic surgery.

C. processing insurance claims.

D. providing family planning.

E. teaching English as a second language.

KEY ISSUE 4

Why Do Services Cluster in Settlements?

Learning Outcome 12.4.1: Describe the difference between clustered and dispersed rural settlements.

A clustered rural settlement is an agricultural-based settlement in which houses are close together. A dispersed rural settlement has isolated individual farms.

Learning Outcome 12.4.2: Explain the types of services in early settlements.

The earliest settlements provided consumer services, especially as places to bury and honor the dead. Early settlements were also places of education and production of tools. Early public services included governance and protection of dependents.

Learning Outcome 12.4.3: Identify important prehistoric, ancient, and medieval urban settlements.

Urban settlements may have originated in Southwest Asia, or they may have originated in multiple hearths. Few people lived in urban settlements until modern times.

Learning Outcome 12.4.4: Explain the two dimensions of urbanization.

Urbanization involves an increase in the percentage of people living in urban settlements. Developed countries have higher percentages of urban residents than do developing countries. Urbanization also involves an increase in size of settlements. Most very large settlements are in developing countries.

A large percentage of the world's population still practice agriculture and live in rural settlements. In **clustered rural settlements**, families live to close to one another and fields surround houses and farm buildings. In **dispersed rural settlements**, farmers live on individual farms and are more isolated from their neighbors.

Circular rural settlements consist of a central open space surrounded by buildings. The medieval German Gewandorf settlements and East African Masai villages are examples of circular settlements. Linear rural settlements are clustered along transportation like roads or rivers. In North America most linear settlements can be traced to the original French longlot or seigneurial pattern.

Dispersed rural settlements are associated with more recent agricultural settlements in the developed world. In some European countries clustered patterns were converted to dispersed settlements. The rural **enclosure movement** that accompanied the Industrial Revolution in Britain is a good example of this transition. It provided greater efficiency in an agricultural world that relied on fewer farmers.

Urbanization is the process by which the population of cities grows, both in *numbers* and *percentage.* Today in MDCs, about three-fourths of the people live in urban areas, compared to about two-fifths in LDCs, although urbanization in Latin America is comparable to MDCs. In MDCs the process of urbanization that began around 1800 has largely ended, because the percentage living in urban areas cannot increase much more. The percentage living in cities in LDCs in recent years has increased because of rural to urban migration. Eight of the 10 most populous cities in the world are currently in LDCs.

The population of urban settlements exceeded that of rural settlements for the first time in human history in 2008. In the 1930s Louis Wirth observed major differences between urban and rural residents. He defined a **city** as a permanent settlement that has three characteristics—large size, high population, and socially heterogeneous people. In the urban world most relationships are contractual and employment is more highly specialized than in rural settlements. In MDCs social distinctions between urban and rural residents has become more blurred than in LDCs because nearly everyone in an MDC is now urban.

Key Issue Revisited

12.4. Who do services cluster in settlements?

- Financial, professional, and other business services cluster disproportionately in large world cities to support the operations of major corporations

- World cities also play major consumer and public service functions

Review Questions

12.4.1. The French long-lot system is an example of a

A. circular rural settlement.

B. linear rural settlement.

C. city structure outside North America.

D. colonial city.

E. dispersed service settlement.

12.4.2. For the past 1,000 years the largest cities have been in

A. France.

B. Russia.

C. China.

D. Iraq.

E. Egypt.

Key Terms

Back offices	Market-area analysis
Basic industries	Multiplier effect
Business services	Nonbasic industries
Central business district (CBD)	Offshore financial services
Central place theory	Periodic markets
City	Postindustrial society
City-state	Primate city
Clustered rural settlement	Primate city rule
Consumer services	Public services
Dispersed rural settlement	Range
Economic base	Service
Enclosure movement	Settlement
Gravity model	Threshold
Hinterland	Urbanization

Think Like a Geographer Activities

You have been hired by McDonald's to locate a new restaurant in your state. What demographic data would you find to support your proposal as to the location of the new restaurant? You might find it useful to go to http://www.census.gov to help you find the necessary information.

Quick Quiz

Fill in the blank.

12.1. _____ has been documented as one of the oldest prehistoric urban settlements and would be found in present day Iraq.

12.2. Ancient urban settlements were established in the Eastern Mediterranean around 2,500 B.C., most notably _____ on the island of Crete.

12.3. The acronym used to describe the financial services sector of jobs in the United States is _____.

12.4. A _____ is the shape most closely associate with Christaller's Central Place Theory.

12.5. Most of the world's major urban areas are found in _____ countries, where as _____ countries have a higher percentage of urban residents.

Free Response

Define and give one example of threshold and range as it applies to services provided in MDCs. Explain and give an example of why some services have a much larger range than others.

On the Web

http://www.masteringgeography.com
http://www.businessdictionary.com/definition/services.html
http://geography.about.com/od/urbaneconomicgeography/a/sectorseconomy.htm
http://www.princeton.edu/~achaney/tmve/wiki100k/docs/Tertiary_sector_of_the_economy.html
http://www.cableready.net/246/thomas-l-friedman-reporting-the-other-side-of-outsourcing/
http://geography.about.com/od/urbaneconomicgeography/a/centralplace.htm

Key Figures

Figure 12-6 Changes in U.S. Employment
Figure 12-9 Why Geographers Use Hexagons to Delineate Market Areas
Figure 12-20 Global Cities
Figure 12-36 Largest Settlements since 1 A.D.

Chapter

13 Urban Patterns

Why Do Services Cluster Downtown?

Urban geographers are concerned with the global distribution of urban settlements as well as the distribution of people and activities within urban areas. This chapter begins by addressing why services cluster downtown. The chapter then examines models that have been developed to help explain the internal structure of urban areas in the North America and elsewhere. The distinctive problems of inner cities and suburbs are also considered.

Learning Outcome 13.1.1: Describe the three types of services found in a CBD.

The CBD contains a large percentage of an urban area's public, business, and consumer services. Offices cluster in the CBD to take advantage of its accessibility. Retail services, as well as manufacturers and residents, are less likely than in the past to be in the CBD.

Learning Outcome 13.1.2: Explain the three-dimensional nature of a CBD.

A CBD is characterized by an extensive underground city of services and utilities, as well as high-rise buildings. Outside North America, CBDs may have more consumer services and fewer high-rise offices.

The **central business district (CBD)** is the center of a city where services have traditionally clustered. Specifically three types of retail services have concentrated in the center because they require accessibility. These include services with a high threshold, those with a long range, and those that serve people who work in the center. A large department store is a service with a high threshold. Retail services with a high range are specialized shops that are patronized infrequently. Both of these types of services have moved in large numbers to suburban locations in recent years. Retailers survive in some CBDs if they combine retailing with recreational activities. This has become a reality in Boston, Baltimore, Philadelphia, and San Francisco. Services that cater to people working in the CBD have remained in this location and have actually expanded, especially where CBDs have been revitalized. Business services such as advertising and banking have also remained clustered in the CBD.

Land costs in the CBD are very high because of competition for accessibility. Thus land use is more intensive in the CBD, and some activities are excluded from the center because of the high cost of space. The built character is more vertical than other parts of urban areas, both above and below ground. Infrastructure, including transportation and utilities, typically run underground. Skyscrapers give the central city its distinctive image. Washington, D.C. is the only large U.S. CBD that does not have skyscrapers because no building is allowed to be higher than the U.S. Capitol dome. High rents and land shortages have excluded industrial and residential activities from the CBDs of North American cities. Industries that have not closed have moved their operations to the suburbs where they can take advantage of cheaper land. Residents have also moved away from CBDs. Pull factors have lured them to the suburbs; the crime and poverty of central cities have acted as a push factor. In the twenty-first century, the population of many U.S. CBDs has increased, largely as a result of urban renewal. "Empty nesters" and young professionals are particularly attracted to downtown living.

European CBDs are visibly very different because they have tried to preserve their historic cores by limiting high-rise buildings. More people live downtown outside North America, but renovation is more expensive and does not always produce enough space to meet the demand. As a result, rents are much higher in the center of European cities than in U.S. cities.

Key Issue Revisited

13. 1. Why do services cluster downtown?

- The central business district (CBD) contains a large percentage of a settlement's business services

- Business services cluster downtown to facilitate face-to-face contact

- Retailers with large thresholds or large ranges may also locate downtown

Review Questions

13.1.1. The oldest area of a city would be found in

A. the zone of transition.

B. the industrial zone.

C. the CBD.

D. the zone of gentrification.

E. the suburbs.

13.1.2. In cities outside the United States more people live

A. in the agricultural zone.

B. in the manufacturing zone.

C. in the suburbs.

D. in rural areas.

E. in the CBD.

KEY ISSUE 2

Where Are People Distributed Within Urban Areas?

Learning Outcome 13.2.1: Describe the concentric zone, sector, and multiple nuclei models.

According to the concentric zone model, a city grows outward in rings. According to the sector model, a city grows along transportation corridors. According to the multiple nuclei model, a city grows around several nodes.

Learning Outcome 13.2.2: Analyze how the three models help to explain where people live in an urban area.

According to the concentric zone model, housing is newer in outer rings than in inner rings. According to the sector model, wealthier people live in different corridors than do poorer people. According to the multiple nuclei model, different ethnic groups cluster around various nodes.

Learning Outcome 13.2.3: Describe how the three models explain patterns in cities outside North America.

In other countries, wealthier people live in different sectors than poorer people, and outer rings have newer housing. In cities outside North America, lower-income people are more likely to live in outer rings.

Learning Outcome 13.2.4: Describe the history of development of cities in developing countries.

Many cities in developing countries are shaped by colonial powers. Since gaining their independence, developing countries have seen cities grow rapidly.

Three different models were developed in Chicago to help explain the internal spatial organization of the urban environment. The **concentric zone model** was developed in 1923 by Burgess and applies to cities that have concentric rings of development emanating outward from a core or **central business district (CBD)**. The ring immediately outside the CBD is a **zone of transition,** containing industry and poorer-quality housing. The rings each contain different kinds of urban land use and residences become more high class further away from the CBD. The underlying sociological concepts of invasion and succession help to explain how people move away from the city center as they become wealthier and are prepared to commute further.

The **sector model** was developed in 1939 by Hoyt who saw the city developing as a series of sectors rather than rings. He believed that certain areas of the city might be more attractive for various activities because of environmental factors. The sectors often followed transportation lines. Hoyt and Burgess both claimed that social patterns in Chicago supported their model.

The **multiple nuclei model** was developed by Harris and Ullman in 1945. They believed that cities lack one central core, and instead have numerous **nodes** of business and cultural activities. Although dated, these models help geographers to understand where different people live in an urban area and why they live there. Cities in MDCs as well as LDCs exhibit characteristics of these models, but no one city matches any model perfectly.

In order to apply these models to reality, accurate data needs to be available. In the United States that information is available from the U.S. Census Bureau which has divided urban areas into **census tracts** that are essentially urban neighborhoods. They provide information about the characteristics of residents living in each tract. Social scientists can compare the distributions of characteristics and create an overall picture of where different people live. This kind of study is known as **social area analysis.**

These three models were developed to describe the spatial distribution of social classes in the urban United States. However they can also be applied to urbanization outside North America. In European cities wealthier people tend to live closer to the CBD, and there is more suburban poverty. European cities are also much older and still retain their medieval city center. In LDCs the poor are also accommodated in the suburbs, whereas the wealthier live near the center of cities. European colonial policies left a heavy mark on the development of cities in LDCs.

Islamic cities, such as Mecca, were laid out surrounding a religious core. They have mosques and a bazaar or marketplace at their center with walls guarding the perimeter. In the outer rings there were secular businesses and quarters laid out for Jews, Christians, and foreigners. Some features of these cities were adaptations to the hot and dry physical environment.

In Asia, Africa, and Latin America cities combine elements of native culture, colonial rule, religion, industry, and poverty. Griffin and Ford developed a model of a **Latin American city**, which shows the wealthy living close to the CBD. Industrial sectors radiate out from the CBD, and the poorest live on the urban fringe in **squatter settlements**. The latter are known by a variety of names such as *barrios, barriadas,* and *favelas* in Latin America, *bidonvilles* in North Africa, and *bustees* in India.

Key Issue Revisited

13.2. Where are people distributed within urban areas?

- The concentric zone, sector, and multiple-nuclei models help to explain where various groups of people live in urban areas

- These models provide a framework for understanding the distribution of social and economic groups within urban areas

- With modifications, the models also apply to cities in Europe and LDCs

Review Questions

13.2.1. Urban areas in the United States are divided by

A. the Department of Homeland Security.

B. the Department of Urban Planning.

C. the Census Bureau.

D. the Population Reference Bureau.

E. the World Health Organization.

13.2.2. In cities like Paris, most of the low-income housing would be found in

A. the suburbs.

B. the CBD.

C. the zone of transition.

D. the industrial area.

E. the gentrified zone.

KEY ISSUE 3

Why Are Urban Areas Expanding?

Learning Outcome 13.3.1: State three definitions of urban settlements.

A city is a legally incorporated entity that encompasses the older portion of the urban area. An urban area includes the city and built-up suburbs. A metropolitan area includes the city, built-up suburbs, and counties that are tied to the city.

Learning Outcome 13.3.2: Describe how metropolitan areas contain many local governments and overlap with each other.

In some regions, adjacent metropolitan areas overlap with each, creating large contiguous urban complexes. The United States has nearly 90,000 local governments, making it difficult to address urban problems.

Learning Outcome 13.3.3:I Identify historical and contemporary patterns of suburban expansion.

In the past, cities expanded their land area to encompass outlying areas, but now they are surrounded by independent suburban jurisdictions. Suburban sprawl has been documented to be costly.

Learning Outcome 13.3.4: Explain two ways in which suburbs are segregated.

Suburbs are segregated according to social class and land uses.

Learning Outcome 13.3.5: Describe the impact of motor vehicles in urban areas.

Motor vehicles take up a lot of space in cities, including streets, freeways, and parking areas. Some cities control the number of vehicles that can enter the center of the city.

Learning Outcome 13.3.6: Describe recent and possible future improvements in vehicles.

Vehicles that are more fuel-efficient and less polluting are likely to become more widely available in the future.

Learning Outcome 13.3.7: State benefits and limitations of public transportation.

Public transit, such as subways and buses, are more suited than private cars to move large numbers of people into and out of the CBD. New investment in public transit has occurred in a number of U.S. cities, though less extensively than in other countries.

North American cities are increasingly following a structure that Harris calls the **peripheral model**. The peripheral model consists of an inner city surrounded by growing suburbs that combine residential and business areas and is tied together by a beltway or ring road. Nodes of business and consumer services called **edge cities** have developed around the beltway. Edge cities have grown from suburbs that were originally primarily residential.

Annexation is the process of legally adding land area to a city. In the United States most surrounding suburban lands have their own jurisdictions and want to remain legally independent of the central city. Instead of annexing peripheral areas, cities are now surrounded by suburbs. As a result, several definitions have been created to characterize cities and their suburbs. In the 1930s Louis Wirth, an urban geographer, defined a **city** as a permanent settlement that has a large size, high population density, and socially heterogeneous people. Urban settlements today can be physically defined by legal boundary, as continuously built-up area, and as a functional area. Virtually all countries have a political system that recognizes cities as legal entities with fixed boundaries. In the United States a city that is surrounded by suburbs is sometimes called a **central city**. The central city and surrounding suburbs are together called an **urbanized area**.

The U.S. Census Bureau defines the functional areas of cities for political and economic purposes. A **Metropolitan Statistical Area (MSA)** includes an urbanized area with a population of at least 50,000 with high density adjacent counties where the majority of inhabitants work in nonagricultural jobs. The census has also designated smaller urban areas as **micropolitan statistical areas**. These include an urbanized area of between 10,000 and 50,000 inhabitants and adjacent counties tied to the city. A **Combined Statistical Area (CSA)** consists of two adjacent MSAs with overlapping commuter patterns such as the Washington-Baltimore CSA. Within a CSA, an MSA that exceeds one million people may be classified as a **Primary Census Statistical Area (PCSA)**. The metropolitan areas of the northeastern United States now form one continuous urban complex or **megalopolis** (from the Greek word meaning great city).

Many urban regional problems cannot be easily solved because of the fragmentation of local government. There are 1,400 local governments in the New York area alone, and 20,000 throughout the United States. Most U.S. metropolitan areas have a **council of governments**, consisting of representatives of the various local governments, and that can do some planning for the entire area. There are two kinds of metropolitan-wide governments. A **federation system** of government combines the various municipalities of a metropolitan area into a single government. Toronto, Ontario has a federation system. Some U.S. cities have consolidated city and county governments. Indianapolis and Miami are both examples of **consolidations.**

In North American urban areas, the further one gets from the center of the city, there will be a decline in the density at which people live. This is called the **density gradient**. The number of houses per unit area of land will decline with distance from the center city. In North American and European cities in recent years, the density gradient has leveled out as more people have moved to the suburbs. **Suburban sprawl** has increased at the expense of agricultural land, and it results in the need for costly infrastructure. Several British cities are surrounded by **greenbelts,** or rings of open space, to prevent suburban sprawl. **Zoning ordinances**, which prevent the mixing of land uses, has resulted in segregated residential suburbs. Residents are separated from industrial and service activities, and poorer residents are excluded because of the cost, size, or location of housing. North American suburbs are no longer just areas of residential growth. Businesses have moved to the suburbs. Retailing has become concentrated in suburban malls. Factories and offices have also moved to suburbia. If they don't require face-to-face contact they can take advantage of the lower rents in the suburbs.

Several U.S. states are passing legislation and regulations called **smart growth**; it limits suburban sprawl and preserves farmland on the urban periphery. Maryland has done an especially good job in this area.

Suburban sprawl has resulted in an increased dependence on transportation, especially motor vehicles in the United States. Public transportation is much more important in most European and Japanese cities. Public transportation in the form of rapid transit is becoming more common in U.S. cities although it is still not recognized as a key utility that needs to be subsidized.

Key Issue Revisited

13.3. Why are urban areas expanding?

- The suburban lifestyle attracts many people

- Transportation improvements, notably the railroad in the nineteenth century and the automobile in the twentieth century, have facilitated the sprawl of urban areas

- Segregation and inefficiency are negative consequences of large-scale sprawl

Review Questions

13.3.1. The largest increase in population within American cities has occurred in

A. the CBD.

B. rural areas.

C. the zone of transition.

D. the manufacturing zone.

E. the suburbs.

13.3.2. A council of governments would most likely be concerned with

A. nuclear disarmament.

B. garbage pick up in megalopolises.

C. education of women.

D. aging populations.

E. environmental destruction.

KEY ISSUE 4

Why Do Cities Face Challenges?

Learning Outcome 13.4.1: Describe the processes of deterioration and gentrification in cities.

The older housing in the inner city can deteriorate through processes of filtering and redlining. Massive public housing projects were once constructed for poor people, but many of them have been demolished. Some cities have experienced gentrification, in which higher-income people move in and renovate previously deteriorated neighborhoods.

Learning Outcome 13.4.2: Explain the problems of a permanent underclass and culture of poverty in cities.

Inner cities have concentrates of very poor people, considered to belong to an underclass, some of whom are homeless. A culture of poverty traps some poor people in the inner cities.

Learning Outcome 13.4.3: Describe the difficulties that cities face in paying for services, especially in a recession.

Cities are faced with the choice of reducing services or raising taxes to pay for needed services. The severe recession that started in 2008 continues to hurt the economic condition of cities. Some cities have seen a revival of retail services downtown.

Inner cities in the United States have a multitude of physical, social, and economic problems. One of the major physical problems is **filtering**, which is when houses are subdivided and occupied by successive waves of lower-income people. It can lead to total abandonment. As a result of filtering inner city neighborhoods have rapidly declining populations. **Redlining** is when banks draw lines on a map to identify areas where they will refuse to loan money although the Community Reinvestment Act has essentially made this illegal.

Governments at various levels have put together grants to help the revitalization of inner-city neighborhoods. This process is called **urban renewal**. Substandard inner-city housing has been demolished and replaced with **public housing** for low-income people. Many of the public high-rise projects built during the 1950s and 1960s have since been demolished because they were considered unsafe. More recently the trend has been to renovate deteriorating inner-city houses so that they will appeal to middle-class people. This process is known as **gentrification**.

There are numerous inner-city social problems too. Many of the residents are considered an **underclass** because they are trapped in a cycle of economic and social problems. Many lack the necessary job skills for even the most basic jobs, and there are more than 3 million homeless in the United States today. This culture of poverty leads to various crimes including drug use, gangs, and other criminal activities.

Most inner-city residents cannot pay the taxes that are necessary to provide public services. A city has two choices to close the gap between the cost of services and the funding available from taxes. It can reduce services and/or raise tax revenues. Federal government contributions have helped, but these have declined substantially since the 1980s. The percentage of the budgets of the 50 largest U.S. cities supplied by the federal government declined to 6 percent in 1990 and 2000. Some state governments have increased financial assistance to cities.

A major cause of the recession that began in 2008 was the collapse in the housing market, primarily in the inner city. Compounding the problem, housing prices have fallen in the United States and other MDCs since their peak in 2006.

Food deserts have begun to emerge in major cities, which compounds the problems of the underclass as they do not have accessibility to healthy foods because they lack transportation and the ability to go to a local supermarket.

Key Issues Revisited

13.4. Why do cities face challenges?

- Inner-city residential areas have physical problems because of older, deteriorating houses

- Inner-city residential areas have social problems as a result of a high percentage of low-income households

- Inner-city residential areas have economic problems stemming from a gap between demand for services and supply of local tax revenue

Review Questions

13.4.1. Which of these are problems faced by cities in the United States?

A. redlining

B. public housing

C. filtering

D. white flight

E. All of these are problems in U.S. cities.

13.4.2. A collapse in the inner city housing market was a major cause of

A. the 2008 recession.

B. outsourcing.

C. the New International Division of Work.

D. "right to work states" being created.

E. the gentrification movement.

Key Terms

Annexation
Central Business District (CBD)
Central city
Census tract
City
Concentric zone model
Combined Statistical Area (CSA)
Consolidations
Council of government
Density gradient
Edge city
Federations
Filtering
Food desert
Gentrification
Ghetto
Greenbelt
Islamic city
Latin American city
Megacity
Megalopolis

Metropolitan Statistical Area (MSA)
Micropolitan statistical area
Multiple nuclei model
Nodes
Peripheral model
Primary Census Statistical Area (PCSA)
Public housing
Redlining
Sector model
Smart growth
Social area analysis
Sprawl
Squatter settlements
Underclass
Urban geography
Urbanization
Urbanized area
Urban renewal
Zone of transition
Zoning ordinance

Think Like a Geographer Activities

Research the impact of urbanization on ground water aquifers and rivers. What are the most common characteristics globally that can be made about the connections between them?

Quick Quiz:

13.1. One common characteristic of all three models of urbanization is that
A. none of them include the suburbs.
B. the CBD is always in the middle.
C. high class housing is always near heavy industry.
D. working class homes were located farthest from the CBD.
E. immigrants live in single-family dwellings.

13.2. An example of a retailer with a high threshold would be a (an)
A. department store.
B. office supply store.
C. shore repair shop.
D. dry cleaners.
E. rapid photocopying store.

13.3. The underground CBD would include all but which of the following?
A. garage
B. loading dock
C. sewer
D. pedestrian passages
E. all of these would be found in an underground CBD

13.4. An example of vertical geography is
A. Mt. Everest.
B. terracing rice paddies.
C. a skyscraper.
D. a subway train.
E. a monument.

13.5. All of the following are ways governments try to reduce the demand to use congested roads EXCEPT
A. tolls.
B. congestion charges.
C. permits.
D. bans on autos.
E. subsidized fuel charges.

Free Response

Define gentrification.
Explain why gentrification might be an alternative to suburban sprawl.
Discuss two reasons why middle class families might be attracted to gentrified zones.

On the Web

http://stats.oecd.org/glossary/detail.asp?ID=2819
http://visibleearth.nasa.gov/view
http://www.bbc.co.uk/schools/gcsebitesize/geography/urban_environments/urban_models_medcs_rev1.sh
tml
http://geography.about.com/od/urbaneconomicgeography/a/Urban-Geography-Models.htm
http://www.nrdc.org/smartgrowth/
http://www.unhabitat.org/documents/SOWC10/R4.pdf

Key Figures

Figure 13-9 Concentric Zone Model
Figure 13-10 Sector Model
Figure 13-11 Multiple Nuclei Model
Figure 13-18 Model of Latin American City
Figure 13-28 Megalopolis
Figure 13-31 Density Gradient in Cleveland
Figure 13-39 Brussels, Belgium, Metro and Tram

AP Human Geography Practice Test 1

Multiple-Choice Section: You have 60 minutes to answer these questions.

Directions: *Choose the one alternative that best completes the statement or answers the question.*

1) Situation identifies a place by its

A) absolute location.
B) mathematical location on Earth's surface.
C) location relative to other places.
D) unique physical characteristics.
E) nominal location.

2) The concept that the distribution of one phenomenon is scientifically related to the location of other phenomena is

A) regional analysis.
B) spatial analysis.
C) spatial association.
D) spatial distribution.
E) relative location.

3) One important feature of the world's population with the most significant future implication is that
A) it is increasing more slowly than in the past.
B) there are more people alive in the world now than at any time in the past.
C) death rates are significantly higher than in the past.
D) people are uniformly distributed across Earth.
E) the most rapid growth is occurring in the developing world.

4) Physiological density is the number of
A) acres of farmland.
B) farmers per area of farmland.
C) people per area of land.
D) people per area suitable for agriculture.
E) people living in a given nation-state.

5) India and the United Kingdom have approximately the same arithmetic density. From this we can conclude that the two countries have the same
A) level of output per farmer.
B) number of people per area of land suitable for agriculture.
C) pressure placed by people on the land to produce food.
D) number of people per area of land.
E) all of the above

6) The medical revolution has been characterized by
A) the invention of new medical technologies.
B) diffusion of medical practices.
C) the elimination of traditional causes of death in developing countries.
D) longer life expectancies in the developing world.
E) all of the above.

7) The lowest natural increase rates are found in countries in which stage of the demographic transition?
A) Stage 1
B) Stage 2
C) Stage 3
D) Stage 4
E) Stages 1 and 2

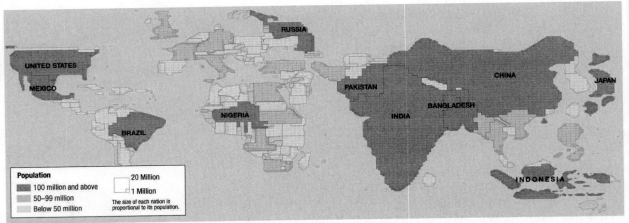

© 2014 Pearson Education, Inc.

8) The map above, which displays countries according to population size rather than land area is a
A) population cartogram.
B) Mercator projection.
C) population pyramid.
D) equal area projection.
E) Robinson projection.

9) Thomas Malthus concluded that
A) population increased geometrically while food production increased arithmetically.
B) the world's rate of population increase was higher than the development of food supplies.
C) moral restraint was producing lower crude birth rates.
D) population growth was outpacing available resources in every country.
E) both A and B.

10) Most people migrate primarily because of which type of push factor?
A) economic
B) environmental
C) political
D) religious
E) all of the above

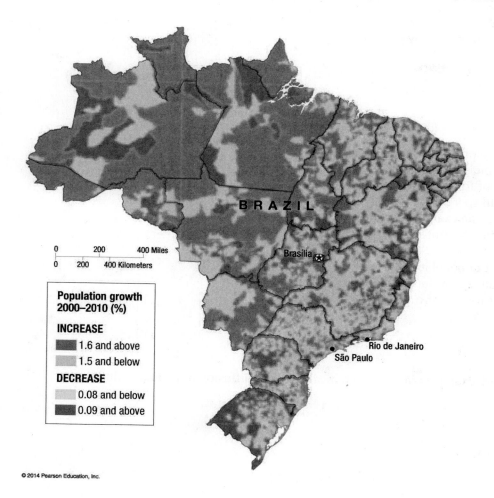

Population growth
2000–2010 (%)

INCREASE
■ 1.6 and above
▪ 1.5 and below

DECREASE
▫ 0.08 and below
■ 0.09 and above

11) The map above shows this type of migration:
A) intraurban.
B) international.
C) interregional.
D) intraregional.
E) interurban.

12) Many Asians are currently migrating to the United States through the process of
A) political asylum.
B) brain drain.
C) chain migration.
D) illegal immigration.
E) brain drain followed by chain migration.

13) Counterurbanization is
A) the move from the urban core to suburban areas.
B) largely international migration.
C) increased migration to rural areas and small towns.
D) the trend of the elderly retiring to rural locations.
E) mostly intrarban.

14) Folk cultures are spread primarily by
A) contagious diffusion.
B) remote diffusion.
C) relocation diffusion.
D) stimulus diffusion.
E) hierarchical diffusion.

15) The current distribution of soccer demonstrates that
A) a folk custom can become part of a popular culture.
B) all sports are examples of folk culture.
C) television has infused all sports into popular culture.
D) American football is also an example of a folk culture.
E) most popular cultures began as obscure folk cultures.

16) One significant impact of popular culture is to
A) create a more varied and less uniform landscape.
B) prevent the diffusion of folk culture.
C) limit access to electronic media.
D) modify the physical environment.
E) all of the above.

17) All of the following are examples of electronic media and the diffusion of popular culture except
A) TV.
B) the Internet.
C) Facebook.
D) McDonald's.
E) Youtube.

18) A literary tradition is
A) a form of a language used for official government business.
B) a collection of sounds that a group of people understands.
C) a collection of languages related to each other.
D) the written form of a language.
E) a form of a language spoken in a particular area.

19) A group of languages that share a common ancestor before recorded history is a
A) dialect.
B) language branch.
C) language tree.
D) language group.
E) language family.

20) A creolized language is
A) extinct.
B) endangered.
C) an isolated language family.
D) a possible prehistoric super family.
E) a mix of indigenous and colonial languages.

21) With respect to the relationship between culture, religion, and the physical environment
A) some religions derive meaningful events from the physical environment.
B) religious ideas may be responsible for some of the changes people make in the physical environment.
C) religion is still an important source of identification for some distinct cultural groups.
D) the origin of most religions is associated with specific places.
E) all of the above are true.

22) A large and fundamental division within a religion is a
A) caste.
B) branch.
C) sect.
D) dialect.
E) denomination.

23) The world's largest universalizing religion is
A) Buddhism.
B) Christianity.
C) Judaism.
D) Islam.
E) Hinduism.

24) The world's largest ethnic religion is
A) Judaism.
B) Daoism.
C) Hinduism.
D) Shintoism.
E) Confucianism.

25) Elements of nationalism include all but
A) common culture.
B) shared attitudes.
C) shared emotions.
D) political structure.
E) all of the above are elements of nationalism.

26) Denmark is the best example of a nation-state because
A) nearly all Danes speak Danish and live in Denmark.
B) Denmark is part of the European Union.
C) the people living on the Faeroe islands, which are controlled by Denmark, speak Faeroese.
D) Danish and German nationalities intermingle in Schleswig-Holstein.
E) all of the above.

27) Balkanization refers to
A) the creation of nation-states in southeastern Europe.
B) a small state inhabited by many ethnic groups.
C) a small geographic area that cannot successfully be organized into states.
D) the breakdown of a state due to conflicts among nationalities.
E) ethnic cleansing.

28) A nation or nationality is
A) a group of people tied together through a common ancestor.
B) a country.
C) ethnic identity.
D) a group of people tied to a place through legal status and personal allegiance.
E) any cohesive group of people.

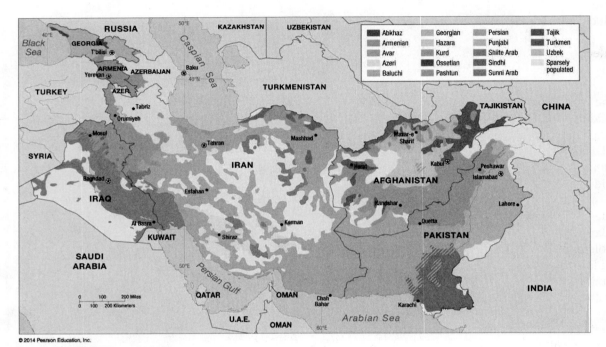

Ethnicities in Western Asia

29) Which of the following can be supported from the above map?
A) Armenia is primarily a homogeneous state
B) There is major conflict between Sunni and Shiite Arabs in Pakistan.
C) Most Kurds in western Asia live in northern Iran.
D) Afghanistan is primarily a homogenous state.
E) Azerbaijan is a compact state.

30) The process when a group forcibly removes another group is called
A) war.
B) apartheid.
C) racism.
D) ethnic cleansing.
E) genocide.

31) One example of a multinational state is
A) United Kingdom.
B) Taiwan.
C) Slovenia.
D) Iceland.
E) Republic of Korea.

32) An area organized into an independent political unit is a
A) colony.
B) sphere of influence.
C) state.
D) protectorate.
E) satellite.

33) The Law of the Sea recognizes ocean boundaries by
A) designating all oceans as the "high seas" with no state control allowed.
B) giving some countries exclusive control of international waters.
C) standardizing the territorial limits for most countries at 200 nautical miles.
D) standardizing the territorial limits for most countries at 12 nautical miles.
E) allowing landlocked countries to claim rights to some international waters.

34) Wasted vote, excess vote, and stacked vote gerrymandering are all examples of
A) the redrawing of political boundaries to provide more electoral equality.
B) the redrawing of legislative boundaries in most European countries.
C) methods of creating electoral districts that are still legal in the United States.
D) the redrawing of political boundaries by a bipartisan commission.
E) the redrawing of legislative boundaries to benefit the party in power.

35) A state with a large projecting extension is a
A) compact state.
B) perforated state.
C) fragmented state.
D) prorupted state.
E) elongated state.

36) The Human Development Index
A) measures the level of development of a country.
B) considers development to be a function of a decent standard of living.
C) considers development to be a function of a long and healthy life.
D) considers development to be a function of access to education.
E) all of the above.

37) An example of a primary sector activity is
A) education.
B) manufacturing.
C) mining.
D) retailing.
E) the processing of raw materials.

38) Compared to more developed countries, less developed countries typically have all but which of the following characteristics?
A) higher crude birth rates
B) lower dependency ratios
C) higher percentage of children under age 15
D) lower percentage of elderly
E) lower life expectancy

39) According to Rostow's development model, the process of development begins when
A) a high percentage of national wealth is allocated to nonproductive activities.
B) an elite group initiates innovative activities.
C) take-off industries achieve technical advances.
D) workers become more skilled and specialized.
E) the economy shifts from production of heavy industry to consumer goods.

40) In contrast to the international trade approach, the self-sufficiency approach to development
A) begins when an elite group initiates innovative activities.
B) results in uneven resource development.
C) suffers from market stagnation.
D) spreads investment through all sectors of the economy.
E) calls for a country to identify its unique economic assets.

41) Alternative energy resources that are renewable include all but which of the following
A) hydroelectric power.
B) solar energy.
C) geothermal energy.
D) nuclear power.
E) wind power.

42) The main features that distinguish commercial agriculture from subsistence agriculture include all of the following except
A) whether the product is consumed on or off the farm.
B) whether crops are grown or animals are raised.
C) the percentage of farmers in the labor force.
D) the use of machinery.
E) farm size.

43) The form of subsistence agriculture that feeds the largest number of people in the developing world is
A) intensive subsistence.
B) shifting cultivation.
C) pastoral nomadism.
D) dairy farming.
E) plantation farming.

44) Pastoral nomadism is most commonly found in which climate region?
A) humid low-latitude
B) dry
C) warm mid-latitude
D) cold mid-latitude
E) marine west coast

45) According to von Thünen's model, a commercial farmer is most concerned with which of these costs?
A) cost of the land
B) cost of transporting output to market
C) value of yield per hectare
D) all of the above
E) A and B only

46) Unlike most other types of agriculture, plantation agriculture is
A) part of agribusiness.
B) a form of subsistence agriculture found in developed countries.
C) a form of commercial agriculture found in developing countries.
D) practiced in much of the world's high-latitude climates.
E) usually situated in densely settled locations.

47) The Industrial Revolution
A) was geographically dispersed.
B) was a transformation that was solely industrial.
C) is a term commonly used to define a process that began in Eastern Europe.
D) was a gradual diffusion of new ideas and techniques.
E) first developed in the United States.

48) Copper production is a bulk-reducing industry because
A) the mills are near the mines.
B) the final product has a much higher value per weight.
C) refineries import most material from other countries.
D) copper ore is low-grade.
E) it involves several steps.

49) Maquiladoras
A) are factories in Mexico near the U.S. border.
B) have become more important since the North American Free Trade Agreement eliminated international trade barriers in the region.
C) take advantage of much lower labor costs in Mexico.
D) are factories built by U.S. companies.
E) All of the above are true.

50) A company that uses more than one mode of transport will often locate near
A) break-of-bulk points.
B) consumers.
C) raw material.
D) major urban areas.
E) their sources of inputs.

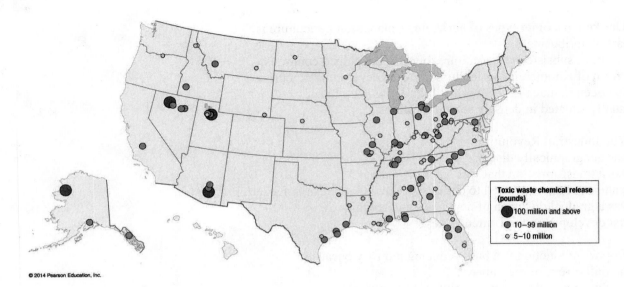

© 2014 Pearson Education, Inc.

51) The above map of toxic chemical release sites shows
A) that most sites are located in the western United States.
B) that toxic waste in the United States is a much bigger problem today than it was 20 years ago.
C) that most sites are located in Georgia.
D) that the largest sites are in the western United States.
E) that the largest sites are mines in Ohio.

52) The Central Business District attracts services primarily because of its
A) geographical size compared to the rest of the urban land area.
B) high land costs.
C) more intensive land use.
D) construction of skyscrapers.
E) accessibility.

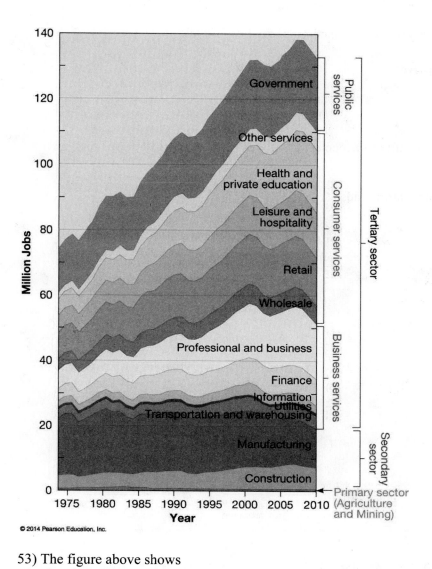

© 2014 Pearson Education, Inc.

53) The figure above shows
A) a huge increase in business services.
B) job increases in the tertiary sector.
C) a huge decline in the secondary sector.
D) a major decline in primary sector jobs.
E) decreases in government services.

54) Rural settlements differ from urban settlements primarily according to which type of activity?
A) cultural
B) economic
C) political
D) religious
E) social

55) Historically, linear rural settlements were developed primarily because of
A) collective land ownership.
B) the need for common grazing land.
C) inheritance laws.
D) the need for access to a river or other means of communication.
E) the need for defense.

56) The most significant anticipated benefit of the enclosure movement in Great Britain was to
A) destroy traditional village life.
B) provide labor for the factory system.
C) replace abandoned villages with new farmsteads.
D) stimulate urbanization.
E) promote agricultural efficiency.

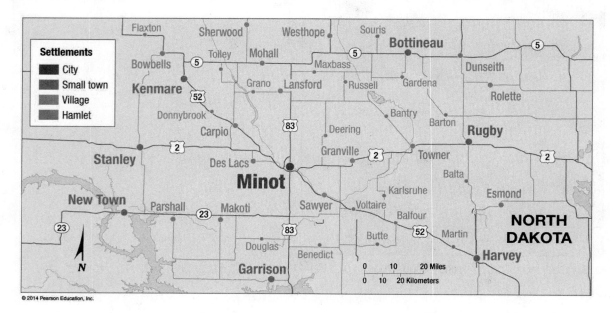

57) What is true of central place theory, shown above?
A) Larger settlements are fewer in number but closer together than smaller market areas.
B) It helps to explain how the most profitable location can be identified.
C) The competition between places creates an irregular pattern of settlements.
D) Squares are used to delineate market areas.
E) The range is the minimum distance people are willing to travel to use a service.

58) The maximum distance people are willing to travel for a service is the
A) hinterland.
B) range.
C) threshold.
D) market area.
E) friction of distance.

59) According to the gravity model, the potential use of a service at a location is related
A) directly to population and inversely to distance.
B) directly to distance and inversely to population.
C) directly to both population and distance.
D) inversely to both distance and population.
E) to none of the above.

60) If a country's largest city has 1,000,000 inhabitants and the second largest city has 200,000 inhabitants, the country follows what distribution?
A) central place theory
B) economic base
C) the primate city rule
D) the rank-size rule
E) the gravity model

61) The urban model that best accounts for the rise of edge cities in North America is the
A) peripheral model.
B) concentric zone model.
C) multiple-nuclei model.
D) sector model.
E) demographic transition model.

62) In the United States, which of the following definitions of a city covers the largest land area?
A) central business district
B) central city
C) suburban area
D) metropolitan statistical area
E) urban cluster

63) The process of change in the use of a house, from single-family owner occupancy to abandonment, is
A) blockbusting.
B) annexation.
C) gentrification.
D) redlining.
E) filtering.

64) Public transit in European cities is relatively extensive because
A) most Europeans can't afford cars.
B) European governments subsidize public transit.
C) urban population density is lower.
D) the central city contains fewer high-rises.
E) most European cities have not suffered from an eroding tax base.

65) According to the concentric zone model, a city develops in a series of
A) corridors.
B) nodes.
C) sectors.
D) rings.
E) a combination of all of the above.

66) According to the sector model, the best housing is located in
A) sectors throughout the urban area.
B) an outer ring surrounding the city.
C) nodes near universities and parks.
D) renovated inner-city neighborhoods.
E) a corridor from downtown to the edge of the city.

67) According to the multiple nuclei model, an airport is likely to attract nearby
A) heavy industries.
B) medium-class residences.
C) shops.
D) pizzerias and bookstores.
E) hotels and warehouses.

68) Compared to the United States, people with social and economic problems in European cities are more likely to be
A) clustered in inner-city neighborhoods.
B) dispersed throughout the city.
C) clustered in remote suburbs.
D) distributed uniformly throughout the urban area.
E) concentrated in central locations.

69) Most nonrenewable energy sources are
A) replaced continually.
B) generally easy to extract.
C) relatively evenly distributed around the globe.
D) both proven and potential reserves.
E) readily available.

70) Urban economic and social geographic challenges in the United States include all of the following except
A) an eroding tax base, especially in inner-cities.
B) a bigger concentration of low-income residents in suburban areas.
C) physical deterioration of neighborhoods as a result of filtering and redlining.
D) the impact of recession.
E) high rates of unemployment, crime, and substance abuse.

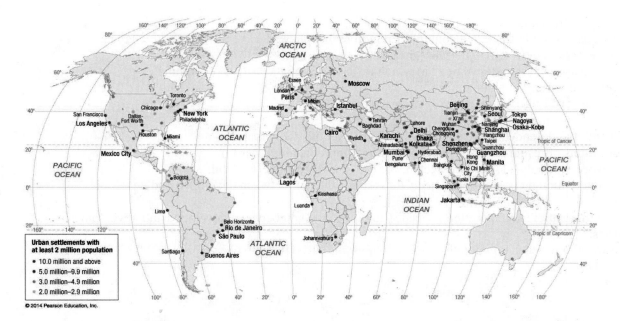

71) According to the above map, most of the world's largest urban settlements are in
A) developed countries.
B) East Asia, especially China and Japan.
C) developing countries.
D) Western Europe.
E) South Asia, especially India.

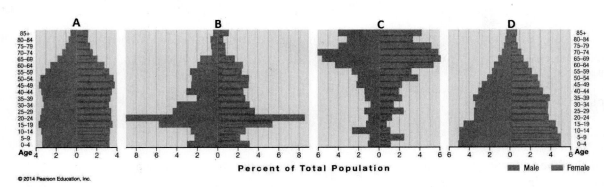

72) Which of the following is a true statement about the population pyramids shown above?
A) Population pyramid D shows a place that has a large percentage of elderly people.
B) Population pyramid B shows a place that has a very high percentage of people in their 20s.
C) Population pyramid A shows a place that has the largest birth rate.
D) These are all population pyramids of developed countries.
E) Life expectancy is relatively low for all these places.

73) A lingua franca is
A) a language used in trade in a country or region by people who have different native languages.
B) a dialect spoken by some African-Americans.
C) a boundary that separates regions in which different language usages predominate.
D) a regional variety of a language.
E) the dialect of English associated with upper-class Britons.

74) Critics and defenders of sustainable development both agree that
A) definitions of resources change drastically and unpredictably over time.
B) the world has only 11.4 billion hectares of biologically productive land.
C) less international cooperation is needed to reduce the gap between developed and developing countries.
D) more international cooperation is needed to reduce the gap between developed and developing countries.
E) the world will reach a population ceiling before the end of the next century.

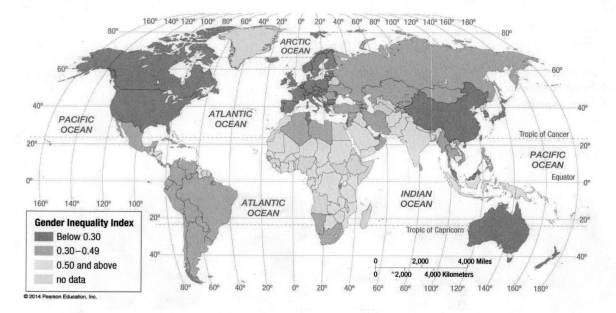

75) Which of the following is shown by the above Gender Inequality (GII) Index map?
A) There is least inequality in Europe.
B) There is most inequality in Asia.
C) There is least inequality in Latin America.
D) The highest GII numbers are in sub-Saharan Africa.
E) Both A and D are true.

End of the multiple-choice portion of the practice test.

Free Response Questions

Directions: *Answer each of the three free response questions in 75 minutes or less.*

1. A. Define the three types of density used in population geography.
    B. Explain why the densities for each country seem to vary significantly.

2. A. Describe the three main types of regimes shown on the below map.
    B. What region of the world seems to have the most autocratic regimes?
    C. Discuss the role of social media in the Arab Spring.

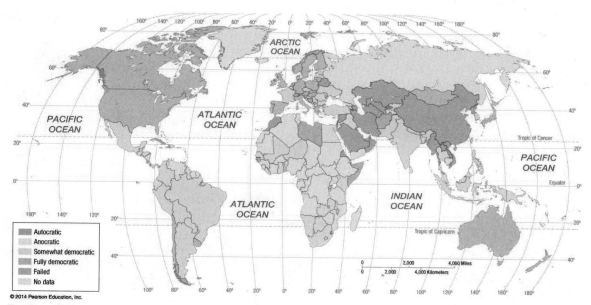

Regime Type

3. A. Diagram the Hoyt Sector Model and Harris and Ullman's Multiple Nuclei Model.
    B. What are the major similarities and differences between the two?
    C. To what extent are these models useful in understanding American urban areas today?

AP Human Geography Practice Test 2

Multiple-Choice Section: You have 60 minutes to answer these questions.

Directions: *Choose the one alternative that best completes the statement or answers the question.*

1. A map is
A. a scale model of the real world.
B. a very accurate model of the real world.
C. an artistic fabrication of the real world.
D. a method of scientific inquiry used to explain the real world.
E. an ancient explanation of the cosmos.

2. The purpose of Ptolemy's *Guide to Geography* was to
A. challenge the Catholic Church.
B. support Isaac Newton's principles.
C. to codify basic principles of mapmaking.
D. to introduce the concept of geography information systems.
E. to compliment the expansion of the Persian Empire.

3. An advantage of a Mercator projection map is
A. shape is distorted very little.
B. landmasses at the poles are very accurate.
C. it is very useful to display information across the oceans.
D. the eastern and western hemispheres are separated.
E. it was developed using GIS technology.

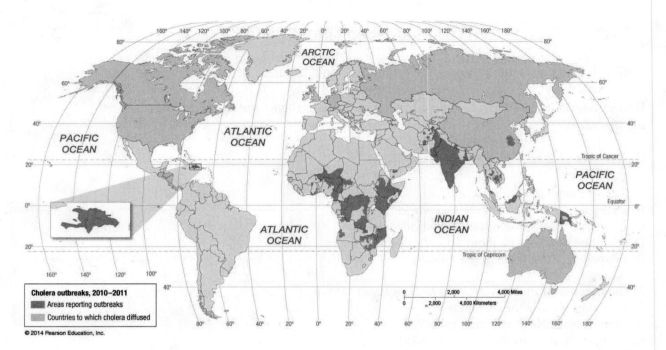

4. Which of the following statements is supported by the above map?
A. Countries reporting cholera in recent years are found primarily in sub-Saharan Africa.
B. Some countries, especially in the developed world, have reported imported cholera cases.
C. Cholera is not a major health concern in South America.
D. Countries reporting cholera in recent years are found primarily in South Asia.
E. All of the above statements are supported by the map.

5. Because Japan is culturally homogeneous, geographers would say it is an example of a
A. functional region.
B. formal region.
C. standard region.
D. vernacular region.
E. perceived region.

6. The three main properties of distribution that geographers look at are
A. density, concentration, and pattern.
B. density, capacity, and concentration.
C. capacity, pattern, and concentration.
D. concentration, density, and dispersement.
E. concentration, capacity, and pattern.

7. To determine a country's farming efficiency, geographers would look at what type of density?
A. agricultural
B. physiological
C. arithmetic
D. concentration
E. clustered

8. The most common measure of population change in a country is determined by looking at
A. crude birth rate, crude death rate, and total fertility rate.
B. crude birth rate, total fertility rate, and life expectancy.
C. crude birth rate, crude death rate, and natural increase rate.
D. natural increase rate, life expectancy, and infant mortality rate.
E. life expectancy, infant mortality rate, and total fertility rate.

9. The dependency ratio shows demographers
A. the number of males per hundred females in the total population.
B. the number of people too young or too old to work.
C. the number of babies born per 1,000 people.
D. the number of children over 15 years old.
E. the number of women between the ages of 15–49.

10. Which contemporary analyst believes that a large population could actually stimulate food production?
A. Garret Hardin
B. Ester Boserup
C. Thomas Malthus
D. Julian Simon
E. Paul Ehrlich

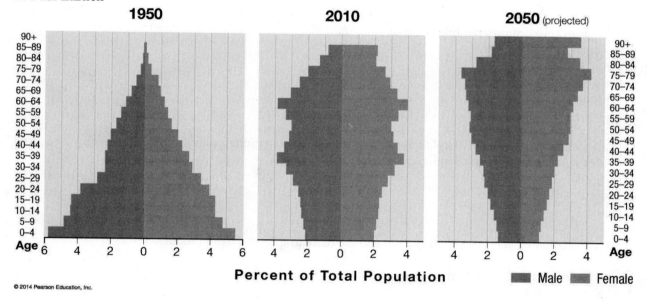

© 2014 Pearson Education, Inc.

11. According to the demographic transition graph above
A. this is a country in stage 1 of the demographic transition model.
B. the birth rate in this country is still increasing.
C. this country is experiencing very high rates of immigration.
D. this is a country in the developing world.
E. this country has a very small gap between birth and death rates.

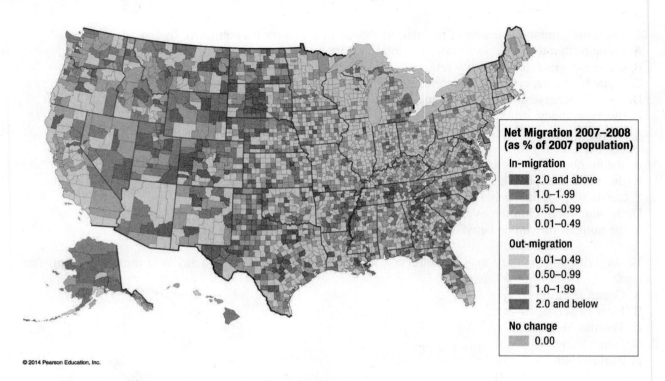

**Net Migration 2007–2008
(as % of 2007 population)**

In-migration
- 2.0 and above
- 1.0–1.99
- 0.50–0.99
- 0.01–0.49

Out-migration
- 0.01–0.49
- 0.50–0.99
- 1.0–1.99
- 2.0 and below

No change
- 0.00

© 2014 Pearson Education, Inc.

12. The map above shows net migration at what scale?
A. regional
B. county
C. state
D. national
E. local

13. According to Wilbur Zelinsky's migration transition, international migration is more likely to occur in countries at what stage of the demographic transition model?
A. Stage 1
B. Stage 2
C. Stage 3
D. Stage 4
E. No correlation exists between migration and the demographic transition model.

14. An intervening obstacle to migration would be
A. U.S. quota laws.
B. family reunification.
C. brain drain.
D. transportation improvements.
E. chain migration.

15. Most immigrants to the United States during the 1840–1850s came from
A. Ukraine and Romania.
B. Austria and Czechoslovakia.
C. Ireland and Germany.
D. Vietnam and Laos.
E. Sweden and Norway.

16. A map showing word usage boundaries uses these to illustrate where one word is most often used:
A. contour lines.
B. isoglosses.
C. lines of latitude.
D. GIS layering.
E. color coding.

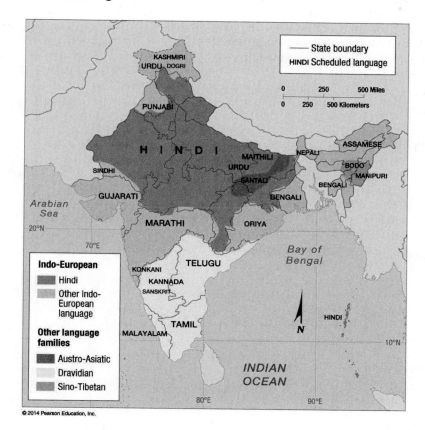

17. According to the above map of language families in India
A. the vast majority of people in India speak Hindi.
B. English is the official language of India.
C. all the languages spoken in India are of the same language family.
D. Sanskrit is the principal language of southern India.
E. although Hindi is the principal language of India, people in the country speak many different languages.

18. The Indo-European language family includes these branches:
A. Indo-Iranian, Austro-Thai, and Germanic.
B. Indo-Iranian, Romance, and Germanic.
C. Indo-Iranian, Romance, and Altaic.
D. Indo-Iranian, Germanic, and Benue-Congo.
E. Indo-Iranian, Proto-Uralic, and Germanic.

19. Hottentots, a language using click clack sounds, is part of what language family?
A. Khoisan
B. Nilo-Saharan
C. Niger-Congo
D. Afro-Asiatic
E. Altaic

20. Why are geographers particularly interested in studying the differences in dialects?
A. They reflect distinctive features of the environments in which groups live.
B. They are a reflection of the influence of globalization on folk cultures.
C. They show how folk cultures affect popular culture.
D. They predict what type of products can successfully be marketed in an area.
E. They are generally confined to English.

21. A universalizing religion would seek to
A. appeal to one group of people.
B. be located in one place.
C. include people from other religions.
D. appeal to all people.
E. include only one cultural group.

22. Which country is comprised of a population that is 90% Shiite?
A. Iraq
B. Iran
C. Pakistan
D. Afghanistan
E. Oman

23. The Baha'i religion was founded in 1844 in
A. Israel.
B. Afghanistan.
C. Pakistan.
D. Iraq.
E. Iran.

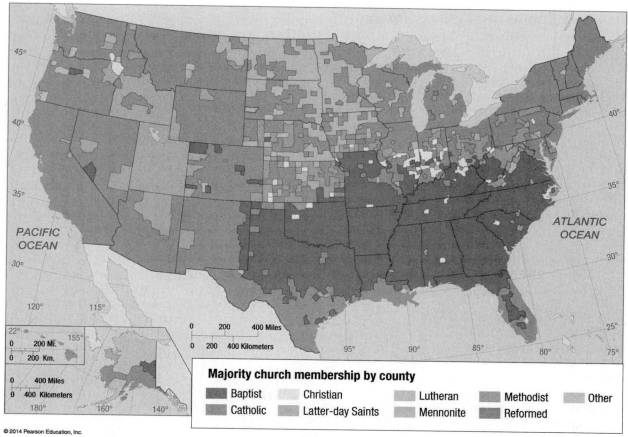

Majority church membership by county
Baptist Christian Lutheran Methodist Other
Catholic Latter-day Saints Mennonite Reformed

© 2014 Pearson Education, Inc.

24. All of the following about the distribution of Christianity in the United States are true except
A. the majority of Christians in the southeastern part of the country are Baptists.
B. the largest number of people in the western United States are Roman Catholic.
C. Utah is predominantly Mormon.
D. New England is predominantly Lutheran.
E. There are only a relatively small number of Mennonites living in the United States.

25. Identity with a group who shares a biological trait is
A. race.
B. ethnicity.
C. nationality.
D. multinationalism.
E. self-determination.

26. In which U.S. state would you find the greatest clustering of Asian Americans?
A. Hawaii
B. Mississippi
C. Texas
D. Maryland
E. Alabama

27. What practice results when real estate agents convince people to sell their homes at low prices?
A. blockbusting
B. redlining
C. white flight
D. gerrymandering
E. desegregation

28. Which is not an example of a centrifugal force?
A. ethnic cleansing
B. racial profiling
C. social classes
D. nationalism
E. indentured servitude

29. Of the following, the best example of an ethnic group divided among many countries are the
A. Croats.
B. Serbs.
C. Kurds.
D. Turks.
E. Druze.

30. The earliest sovereign states that comprised a town together with the surrounding countryside were known as
A. nation-states.
B. nations.
C. countries.
D. colonies.
E. city-states.

31. Which of these states has a unitary system of government?
A. France
B. Russia
C. the United States
D. Brazil
E. India

32. The Human Development Index (HDI) includes which of the following factors in order to determine a country's level of development?
A. GDP, literacy rate, total fertility rate, educational level
B. GDP, life expectancy, total fertility rate, literacy rate
C. GDP, life expectancy, literacy rate, educational level
D. GDP, literacy rate, educational level, net emigration
E. GDP, life expectancy, educational level, net emigration

33. In what region of the world is the HDI significantly lower because females do not have access to educational opportunities?
A. Central Asia
B. Southwest Asia
C. Latin America
D. Southeast Asia
E. Oceania

34. Shifting cultivation takes place mainly
A. in the tropics.
B. in the high latitudes.
C. in arid regions.
D. in rugged mountains.
E. in the temperate zone.

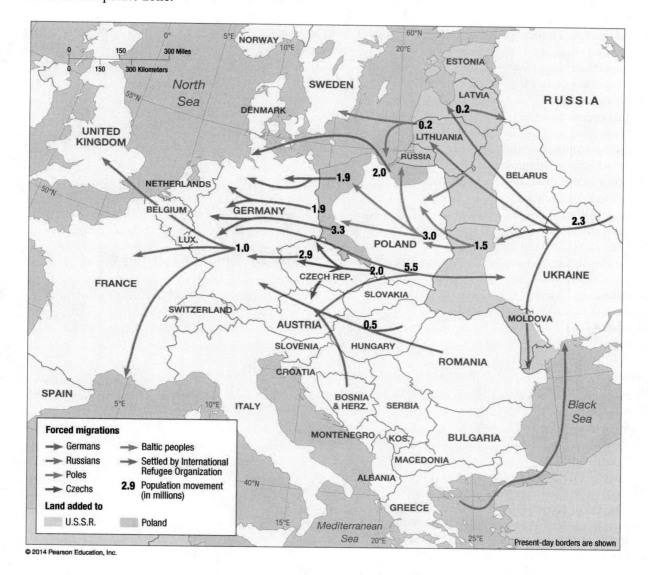

35. The above map shows forced migration after World War Two. Which of the following statements is true about these migrations?
A. The largest migration streams were from eastern to western Europe.
B. There were important migration streams from northern to southern Europe.
C. Most of this migration was mandated by the United Nations.
D. Many people moved to Scandinavia.
E. Large numbers of people left the Balkans after World War II.

36. One of the main characteristics of mixed crop and livestock farming is
A. the effort to grow crops is not uniform throughout the year.
B. most crops grown are for human consumption.
C. it is generally referred to as truck farming.
D. crops are fed to animals rather than consumed by humans.
E. the farm must be closer to the market because the products are highly perishable.

37. In the von Thunen agricultural land use model, animal grazing would most likely be found in
A. the first ring.
B. the second ring.
C. the market center.
D. the third ring.
E. the outermost ring.

38. Some commercial farms are converting to sustainable agriculture, which is distinguished by
A. sensitive land management.
B. better integration of crops and livestock.
C. limited chemicals.
D. ridge tillage.
E. all of the above.

39. In the concentric zone model, most low-income people would find affordable housing in
A. zone 1.
B. zone 2.
C. zone 3.
D. zone 4.
E. zone 5.

40. The process of limiting suburbs and preserving agricultural land is known as
A. redlining.
B. smart growth.
C. suburbanization.
D. gentrification.
E. sprawl.

41. The type(s) of distortion that can occur on a map of the world is/are
A. shapes appear more elongated than they really are.
B. distance between two points may become more increased or decreased.
C. the relative size of areas might be altered.
D. direction from one place to another can be distorted.
E. all of the above.

42. The four ways geographers use to identify a location on Earth are
A. place name, site, situation, toponym, and grid coordinates.
B. toponym, relative location, grid coordinates, and place names.
C. place name, site, situation, and grid coordinates.
D. grid coordinates postal address, site, and situation.
E. postal address, grid coordinates, place name, and site.

43. The cultural traits most often looked at in identifying a culture's location and global distribution are
A. language, religion, and ethnicity.
B. language, religion, and GNP.
C. language, ethnicity, and literacy rate.
D. language, ethnicity, and GNP.
E. religion, ethnicity, and literacy rate.

44. In studying the elk population in Rocky Mountain National Park, geographers would be most interested in what type of density?
A. agricultural
B. physiological
C. arithmetic
D. concentration
E. clustered

45. The geometric arrangement of objects in space is known as
A. pattern.
B. concentration.
C. density.
D. sustainability.
E. dispersement.

46. Which demographic measure most affects the doubling time of a country?
A. natural increase rate
B. total fertility rate
C. infant mortality rate
D. literacy rate
E. life expectancy

47. Which economist predicted that population was growing more rapidly than food supply?
A. Garret Hardin
B. Ester Boserup
C. Thomas Malthus
D. Julian Simon
E. Paul Ehrlich

48. According to Wilbur Zelinsky's migration transition, internal migration occurs more often in countries at what stage of the demographic transition model?
A. Stage 1
B. Stage 2
C. Stage 3
D. Stage 4
E. Both Stage 3 and Stage 4 countries

49. The extinction of the Gothic language was a result of
A. chain migration.
B. relocation diffusion.
C. political dominance and conversion.
D. contagious diffusion.
E. popular culture revival.

50. The three major branches of Christianity include
A. Roman Catholic, Coptic Church, and Eastern Orthodox.
B. Roman Catholic, Armenian, and Protestant.
C. Roman Catholic, Protestant, and Latter Day Saints.
D. Roman Catholic, Protestant, and Eastern Orthodox.
E. Roman Catholic, Protestant, and Maronite.

51. The majority of Sikhs are located in which region of India?
A. Punjab
B. Bangalore
C. Delhi
D. Ganges
E. Bengali

52. Daoism (Taoism) is an ethnic religion based on the teachings of
A. Buddha
B. Confucius
C. Meiji
D. Shakti
E. Lao Zi

53. The single feature of a person's race that geographers are most concerned with is
A. eye color.
B. hair color.
C. blood type.
D. skin color.
E. body type.

54. Identity with a group who share the cultural traditions of a particular hearth is
A. race.
B. ethnicity.
C. nationality.
D. multinationalism.
E. self-determination.

55. In which U. S. State would you find the greatest clustering of Hispanic Americans?
A. Hawaii
B. Mississippi
C. Texas
D. Maryland
E. Alabama

56. Identity with a group of people who share a legal attachment to a country is
A. race.
B. ethnicity.
C. nationality.
D. multinationalism.
E. self-determination.

57. Which country shape could potentially suffer the most from isolation?
A. compact
B. prompted
C. fragmented
D. elongated
E. perforated

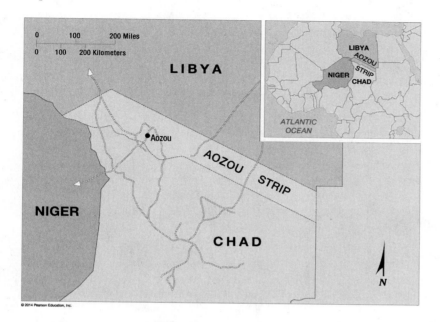

58. The boundary between Chad and Libya, shown on the map above, is an example of a
A. physical boundary.
B. cultural boundary.
C. ethnic boundary.
D. geometric boundary.
E. language boundary.

59. Political unity in the ancient world reached its height under the
A. Roman Empire.
B. Greek Empire.
C. Persian Empire.
D. Mongol Empire.
E. British Empire.

60. The process of redrawing legislative boundaries is
A. blockbusting.
B. redlining.
C. segregation.
D. desegregation.
E. gerrymandering.

61. According to the Human Development Index (HDI), the lowest ranking countries in the world would be found in which region?
A. Central Asia
B. Sub-Saharan Africa
C. South Asia
D. Latin America
E. Southeast Asia

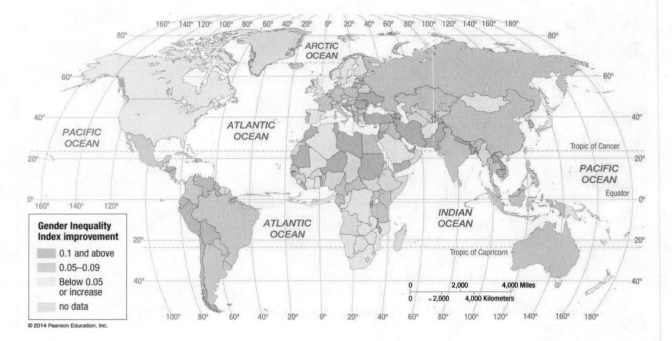

62. Which of the following generalizations can be made from the above map?
A. Most countries in Latin America have shown a decline in their Gender Inequality Index in recent years.
B. Most countries in the developing world have shown little change in their Gender Inequality Index in recent years.
C. Gender inequality has declined significantly in the United States.
D. Women have achieved near-equality with men in Southwest Asia.
E. The percentage of women attending college has grown significantly in most countries.

63. Which three principal features distinguish commercial agriculture from subsistence agriculture?
A. purpose of farming, percentage of farmers in the labor force, and relationship of farming to other businesses
B. purpose of farming, percentage of farmers in the labor force, and farm size
C. purpose of farming, percentage of farmers in the labor force, and agribusiness
D. purpose of farming, percentage of farmers in the labor force, and use of machinery
E. percentage of farmers in the labor force, use of machinery, and farm size

64. Which international organization seeks economic and cultural cooperation among former British colonies?
A. the European Union
B. the North Atlantic Treaty Organization
C. the Commonwealth
D. the Organization on Security and Cooperation in Europe
E. the Council for Mutual Economic Assistance

65. A characteristic of commercial gardening and fruit farming is
A. the effort to grow crops is not uniform throughout the year.
B. most crops grown are for human consumption.
C. it is generally referred to as truck farming.
D. crops are fed to animals rather than consumed by humans.
E. the farm must be closer to the market because the products are highly perishable.

66. Von Thunen maintained that timber for construction and fuel would be found in
A. the first ring.
B. the second ring.
C. the city center.
D. the third ring.
E. the outermost ring.

67. The earliest crops were first domesticated in which agricultural hearth?
A. Southwest Asia
B. East Asia
C. Sub-Saharan Africa
D. Latin America
E. all of the above

68. A Post-Fordist strategy of production differs from that of a Fordist because
A. Post-Fordist are skilled workers who are encouraged to work in teams to achieve a common goal.
B. Post-Fordist work in a large factory where laborers are skilled for only one task.
C. Fordist are focused only on primary sector jobs.
D. Fordist are skilled workers encouraged to work in tarns to achieve a common goal.
E. Post-Fordist are unskilled, cheap laborers.

69. When geographers look at urban settlements, they often refer to a functional area with a county containing a city, where a large percentage of workers are employed as a
A. city.
B. county seat.
C. micropolitan area.
D. metropolitan statistical area.
E. census tract.

70. While using the concentric zone model, you would find most commuters living in
A. Zone 1.
B. Zone 2.
C. Zone 3.
D. Zone 4.
E. Zone 5.

71. The process of converting a low-income renter neighborhood into a middle-class owner neighborhood is
A. redlining.
B. smart growth.
C. suburbanization.
D. gentrification.
E. sprawl.

72. According to the peripheral model, an inner city and the surrounding suburbs are tied together by
A. a ring road.
B. interstate highways.
C. a system of walking paths.
D. major rail links.
E. a bus route.

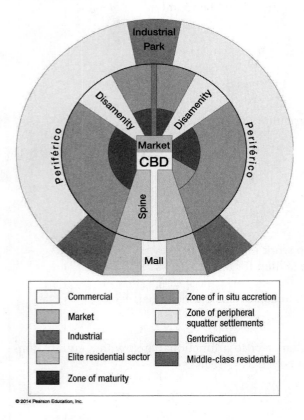

73. The model of a Latin American city shown above is different from models of American cities in that
A. it doesn't have a central business district.
B. it shows that different types of people live in distinctive parts of the city.
C. it is a simplification of urban reality.
D. poorer people live on the outskirts of the urban area.
E. it has a gentrification zone.

74. Fred Kniffen considers the house to be a reflection of
A. cultural heritage.
B. current fashion.
C. functional needs.
D. environmental impact.
E. all of the above.

75. A structural adjustment program includes all of the following except
A. fiscal transparency.
B. direct benefits to the poor.
C. increasing government spending.
D. governmental reform.
E. spending within a country's means.

End of the multiple-choice portion of the practice test.

Free Response Questions

Directions: *Answer each of the three free response questions in 75 minutes or less.*

1. Use the table below to respond to the following free response question.

A. In terms of development, describe the characteristics of economic development in countries at each stage of these transitions.
B. Identify a particular country that meets the criteria for Stages 2–4 of the transitions; explain what criteria makes your choice a viable one.

Stage	Demographic Transition	Migration Transition
1	Low NIR, high CBR, high CDR	High daily or seasonal mobility in search of food
2	High NIR, high CBR, rapidly declining CDR	High international emigration and interregional migration from rural to urban areas
3	Declining NIR, rapidly declining CBR, declining CDR	High international immigration and intraregional migration from cities to suburbs
4	Low NIR, low CBR, low CDR	Same as stage 3

© 2014 Pearson Education, Inc.

2. Call centers are the fastest growing service industry in the world.
A. Define and explain the purpose and function of a call center.
B. Describe where call centers would most likely be located.

3. Use the figure below to respond to the following free response question.

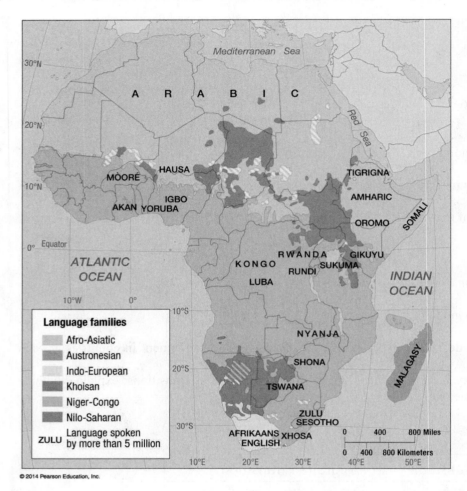

© 2014 Pearson Education, Inc.

Geographers look at centripetal and centrifugal forces when they are trying to determine why countries have conflicts with or cooperate with one another.

A. With regards to Africa, give one example where language acts as a centripetal force.

B. What is one example from the map where language is possibly a centrifugal force?

Answer Key to AP Human Geography Practice Test 1

Multiple Choice Answers Explained

1.**C.** The other choices deal with absolute location and site.

2. **C.** Spatial association identifies cultural, economic, and environmental factors that display similar distributions.

3. **E.** More than 95% of the natural increase is clustered in developing countries. This has significant future implications.

4. **D.** Physiological density is the number of people per area suitable for agriculture.

5. **D.** Arithmetic density is total number of objects in an area, so it tells us nothing more than the number of people per area of land.

6. **E.** All of these statements are true.

7. **D.** By the time countries reach stage 4 they have very low rates of natural increase. For example, this is true of western European countries today.

8. **A.** See Figure 2-2 on page 45. This is a population cartogram, which displays countries by size of population rather than land area.

9. **E.** The statements in A and B are the two basic premises of Malthus's prediction regarding future world population.

10. **E.** There are a wide variety of push factors associated with migration.

11. **C.** See Figure 3-17 on page 89. This map shows migration from one region to another in China. This is interregional migration.

12. **E.** An increasing trend with migration from Asia to the United States is brain drain followed by chain migration. This allows well-educated Asians to take advantage of the priorities set by the U.S. quota laws.

13. **C.** Counterurbanization, which is becoming more common in the United States, is the migration from urban areas to rural areas and small towns. It results in part from very rapid expansion of suburbs.

14. **C.** Unlike popular culture, folk culture is transmitted from one location to another more slowly and on a smaller scale, primarily through relocation diffusion.

15. **A.** Soccer originated as a folk culture in England, and has since been transformed into a part of global popular culture.

16. **D.** Popular culture tends to create a more uniform environment, and provides access to electronic media. It wouldn't necessarily prevent the diffusion of folk culture, and it certainly modifies the physical environment.

17. **D.** All of the others are examples of electronic media and the diffusion of popular culture.

18. **D.** A literary tradition is the written form of a language.

19. **E.** A language family is a collection of languages related through a common ancestral language that existed long before recorded history.

20. **E.** A creolized language is one that results from the mixing of a colonizer's language with the indigenous language of the people being dominated.

21. **E.** All of these statements about the relationship between culture, religion, and the physical environment are true.

22. **B.** Denomination and sect are terms that refer to smaller divisions within a religion.

23. **B.** A universalizing religion is global and seeks to appeal to all people regardless of culture or location. Christianity has more than 2 million adherents, more than any other universalizing religion.

24. **C.** An ethnic religion is one that is relatively geographically concentrated, and likely to be based on the physical characteristics of a particular location. Hinduism is by far and away the world's largest ethnic religion, with more than 900 million adherents.

25. **E.** Nationalism is loyalty and devotion to a particular nationality, and all of these statements are legitimate elements of nationalism.

26. **A.** A nation-state is a state whose territory corresponds to that occupied by a particular ethnicity. Nearly 90% of the population of Denmark consists of ethnic Danes.

27. **D.** The word comes from the Balkans region of South Eastern Europe where there has been so much national and ethnic conflict. It is the process by which a state breaks down through conflicts among its ethnicities

28. **D.** Nationality is identity with a group of people that share legal attachment and personal allegiance to a particular place as a result of being born there.

29. **D.** See Figure 7-34 on page 244. This is the only statement that can be supported from that map. Afghanistan is clearly a multiethnic state.

30. **D.** Ethnic cleansing is the forcible removable of one group by another ethnic group, and it may sometimes involve genocide.

31. **A.** The United Kingdom consists of England, Wales, Scotland, and Northern Ireland. The other countries listed are nation-states.

32. **C.** All of the other options involve some level of dependence.

33. **D.** The Law of the Sea was initially signed by 158 countries, and standardized the limits for most countries at 12 nautical miles.

34. **E.** Gerrymandering was named for Elbridge Gerry, an early nineteenth-century American politician from Massachusetts. It is the redrawing of legislative boundaries to benefit the party in power. It is illegal today.

35. **D.** Proruptions are large projecting extensions of states, and are usually created to provide access to a resource, or to separate two states that otherwise would share a boundary. Namibia is a good example of a prorupted state.

.

36. **E.** All of these statements are true of the Human Development Index.

37. **C.** A primary sector activity is the part of the economy concerned with the direct extraction of materials from Earth's surface, and includes agriculture, mining, fishing, and forestry

38. **B.** The dependency ratio is 47% in Europe, compared to 85% in sub-Saharan Africa. All of the other statements about less developed countries are true.

39. **B.** According to Rostow's development model, the process of development begins in stage 2, which he called "Preconditions for Takeoff." At that time an elite group will initiate innovative economic activities.

40. **E.** In the self-sufficiency model, countries encourage domestic production of goods, and discourage opening themselves up to foreign investment and international markets.

41. **D.** Nuclear power is not renewable. All of the others mentioned are renewable.

42. **B.** Whether crops are grown or animals are raised has nothing to do with the distinction between commercial and subsistence agriculture. All of the other options are features that help to make that distinction.

43. **A.** Intensive subsistence agriculture tries to produce the maximum feasible yield from a parcel of land. It is the form of agriculture that feeds most people in the developing world.

44. **B.** Pastoral nomadism is a form of subsistence agriculture based on the herding of domesticated animals. It is adapted to dry climates, where planting crops is impossible.

45. **E.** According to this model, when choosing an enterprise, the farmer compares two costs: the cost of the land and the cost of transporting products to market.

46. **C.** Plantation agriculture is the most important form of commercial agriculture in the developing world.

47. **D.** The Industrial Revolution was a gradual diffusion of new ideas and techniques that began in western Europe, especially Britain, in the late 1700s.

48. **B.** A bulk-reducing industry in one in which the final product weighs less or comprises a lower volume than the inputs. Copper production is an especially good example of this.

49. **E.** All of these statements about maquildora plants are true.

50. **A.** Break-of-bulk points are locations where transfer is possible from one mode of transportation to another.

51. **D.** The map shows that the largest toxic chemical release sites in the United States are in the west, and these are mostly mines.

52. **E.** Accessibility attracts services to the Central Business District. None of the other options do that.

53. **B.** See Figure 12-6 on page 433. The tertiary sector has grown rapidly in recent years.

54. **B.** Urban settlements are centers for consumer and business services, whereas rural settlements are centers for agriculture and provide a small number of services.

55. **D.** Linear rural settlements comprise buildings clustered along a road, river, or dike to facilitate communications.

56. **E.** The purpose of the enclosure movement was to promote agricultural efficiency, by consolidating small landholdings into a smaller number of large farms in England during the eighteenth century.

57. **B.** See Figure 12-12 on page 437. Central place theory helps to explain how the most profitable location can be identified. None of the other statements are true of central place theory.

58. **B.** The range is the maximum distance people are willing to travel to use a service. The range is the radius of the circle (or hexagon) drawn to delineate a service's market area.

59. **A.** The gravity model holds that the potential use of a service at a particular location is directly related to the number of people in a location and inversely related to the distance people must travel to reach the service.

60. **C.** The primate city rule is when the largest settlement in a country has more than twice as many people as the second-ranking settlement. Argentina and the Republic of Korea are examples of countries that follow this rule.

61. **A.** The peripheral model is a model of North American urban areas consisting of an inner city surrounded by large suburban residential and business areas (including edge cities) tied together by a beltway or ring road.

62. **D.** A metropolitan statistical area in the United States is an urbanized area of at least 50,000 people, the county within which the city is located, together with adjacent counties that have a functional connection to the central city.

63. **E.** Filtering is a process of change in the use of a house, from single-family owner occupancy to abandonment.

64. **B.** In major European cities extensive networks of bus, tram, and subway lines have been maintained, and government funds for new construction have been provided in recent years.

65. **D.** The concentric zone model is a model of the internal structure of cities in which social groups are spatially arranged in a series of rings.

66. **E.** According to the sector model, a city develops in a series of sectors. The best housing, according to the model, is found in a corridor extending from downtown to the outer edge of the city.

67. **E.** The multiple nuclei theory states that some activities are attracted to particular nodes. For example, an airport may attract hotels and warehouses.

68. **C.** Some European policies to help preserve the countryside from development and avoid the sprawl that characterizes American suburbs have resulted in the clustering of people with social and economic problems in high-density and remote suburbs.

69. **B.** Remaining supplies of nonrenewable energy, especially fossil fuels, are both proven and potential reserves. They are unevenly distributed around the globe, and increasingly difficult to extract.

70. **B.** In U.S. metropolitan areas, low-income residents are still largely concentrated in inner-city areas.

71. **C.** See Figure 12-38 on page 455. Most of the world's largest urban settlements are in developing counties.

72. **B.** This is the only true statement that can be made from the population pyramids shown.

73. **A.** B, C, D, and E are definitions of Ebonics, Isogloss, Dialect, and British Received Pronunciation respectively.

74. **D.** Sustainable development is development that meets the needs of people in the present, without compromising the ability of future generations to meet their needs. It can only be effectively achieved through international cooperation.

75. **E.** See Figure 9-17 on page 310. The Gender Inequality Index map shows the least inequality in Europe and the most inequality in sub-Saharan Africa.

Free Response Questions Explained:

1.A. The three types of density used in population geography are arithmetic, physiological, and agricultural. Arithmetic density is simply the total number of people per square kilometer (or unit of land). Physiological density is the number of people who are supported by a unit of arable land. Last agricultural density is the number of farmers per unit of arable land.

B. The reason that the charts vary so much is that countries like the United States and Canada contain so much land area, that when you divide the land area with the population they have a very small arithmetic density compared to the Netherlands which has many people per unit of land because it is so small in land area. Also Egypt is mainly a desert, so it's physiological and agricultural density are very high because it has very little arable land, so the little farmland it has must support many people. Likewise, it is still a country with little agricultural technology, so farmers are mainly subsistent farmers, so many farmers must farm small areas of arable land, compared to Canada or the United States where there is a very small agricultural density.

2. A. The different types of regimes shown on the map are autocratic, which is a country run by ruler who makes decisions based on his/her self interests, an anocracy, which is not autocratic, nor is it a democracy, but rather somewhere in between, and a democracy, where citizens vote to elect leaders and can participate in elections. All three vary according to the selection process of their next leader, the degree to which citizens may participate, and the systems of checks and balances that they may have.

B. By looking at the map, it appears that there is a high concentration of autocratic regimes in the area of North Africa and the Middle East.

C. As the Arab Spring began in 2010, the use of social media played a key role in getting information out to the world through rapid diffusion via Facebook and Twitter. The world watched as the revolutions and regime shifts took place.

3. A. See Figures 13-10 and 13-11 for diagrams of the models.

B. The Hoyt sector model has only five sectors for a city, where as the Multiple Nuclei has nine. Each shows the CBC near a central point and both has middle-class residential next to the CBD. Low-class residential is also next to the CBD in both models. The main difference in the models is that the Multiple Nuclei has many more sectors than the Hoyt model. The Multiple Nuclei breaks down manufacturing into light versus heavy and most importantly includes suburbs, which the Hoyt model does not.

C. Both models can still be used in looking at American urban areas today. For the Hoyt Sector Model, cities still develop along transportation hubs and low income housing can be found near these areas. The Multiple Nuclei Model increasingly becomes relevant as you have suburbanization and many different "mini" CBDs seem to emerge outside of larger cities. The CBD is now no longer the focal point as it once was in the 1950s.

Answer Key to AP Human Geography Practice Test 2

Multiple Choice Answers Explained

1. **A.** A map is a two-dimensional or flat-scale model of Earth's surface, or a portion of it.

2. **C.** Ptolemy collected data from Roman soldiers to prepare maps, many of which were not improved upon for thousands of years.

3. **A.** The biggest disadvantage of a Mercator projection is that the higher latitudes appear much larger than they actually are.

4. **E.** See Figure 2-31 on page 65.

5. **B.** Formal regions are also called uniform or homogenous regions.

6. **A.** Density, concentration, and pattern are the three properties of distribution.

7. **A.** Agricultural density is the number of farmers per unit area of farmland. Countries with a higher agricultural density use less agricultural technology and are in the developing world.

8. **C.** The difference between the crude birth rate and the crude death rate is the rate of natural increase (or decrease). This does not take into account immigration or emigration.

9. **B.** This compares the number of people too young or too old to work with those in their productive years.

10. **B.** Ester Boserup and Simon Kuznets believed that population growth generated more customers and more ideas from improving technology to produce more food.

11. **D.** See Figure 2-18 on page 56. These are the demographic data for Cape Verde, a country in stage 2 of the demographic transition with a large gap between birth and death rates. It is still very much a developing country.

12. **B.** The map shows net in-migration by county.

13. **B.** Internal migration is more important in countries at Stage 3 and 4.

14. **A.** An environmental or political feature that hinders migration is an intervening obstacle. U.S. quota laws are an example of a selective immigration policy that admits some types of immigrants but not others.

15. **C.** Economic push factors, especially the Irish potato famine, and political instability in Germany forced people to leave these countries.

16. **B.** An isogloss is a word usage boundary.

17. **E.** See Figure 5-11 on page 151.

18. **B.** See Figure 5-9 on page 150. These are three of the most widely spoken Indo-European branches.

19. **A.** Refer to Figure 5-8 on page 149. Upon hearing the clicking sounds, whites in southern Africa derisively and onomatopoeically named this language Hottentot.

20. **A.** A dialect is a regional variation of a language distinguished by distinctive vocabulary, spelling, and pronunciation.

21. **D.** A universalizing religion is global and seeks to appeal to all people regardless of culture or location.

22. **B.** The majority of Muslims are Sunnis but the vast majority of Muslims in Iran are Shiite.

23. **E.** It grew out of the Babi faith founded by Siyyid 'Ali Muhammad known as the Bab.

24. **D.** See Figure 6-7 on page 187.

25. **A.** Race is identity with a group of people descended from a biological ancestor.

26. **A.** Asian Americans make up 40% of the population of Hawaii.

27. **A.** This practice perpetuated white flight from the cities.

28. **D.** Centrifugal forces break people apart, whereas centripetal forces, like nationalism, bring them together.

29. **C.** There are large numbers of Kurds in Turkey, Iraq, and Iran. There are not large numbers of the other ethnic groups in more than one country.

30. **E.** This was especially true of Mesopotamia and Greece.

31. **A.** All of the other choices are federal states.

32. **C.** Emigration and fertility rate are not part of the HDI. This index is used by the United Nations.

33. **B.** The literacy rate among females is the main reason the United Nation's HDI index is low in this petroleum rich region.

34. **A.** It is practiced by roughly 250 million people, predominantly in tropical regions.

35. **A.** See Figure 7-37 on page 246.

36. **D.** This is an important type of farming in the developed world. It is the most common form of commercial agriculture in much of the United States and Europe.

37. **E.** *The Isolated State* was written in 1826 to explain that commercial farmers compare the cost of land versus the cost of transportation when deciding what to grow and where to grow it.

38. **E.** This agricultural practice preserves and enhances environmental quality.

39. **B.** Zone 2 is known as the zone of transition where industry and poor quality housing are found.

40. **B.** Most smart growth is due to legislation and regulation.

41. **E.** These four types of distortion can result, and are especially severe for maps depicting the entire world.

42. **C.** Situation is often referred to as relative location, and grid coordinates is the same as absolute location.

43. **A.** GNP and literacy rate are more associated with levels of development.

44. **C.** Arithmetic density is the total number of objects in an area.

45. **A.** Density, concentration, and pattern are the three properties of distribution.

46. **A.** Natural increase is the difference between the crude birth rate and the crude death rate.

47. **C.** Malthus' "An Essay of the Principle of Population" was published in 1798. He believed that the world's population was increasing geometrically whereas food supply was only increasing arithmetically.

48. **E.** International migration occurs most in Stage 2 countries.

49. **C.** Many descendants of the Goths switched to speaking Latin when they converted to Christianity.

50. **D.** Christianity, which is a universalizing religion, is divided into branches, then denominations.

51. **A.** Approximately 20 million Sikhs are clustered in the Punjab. When British India became independent after World War Two, Punjab fought to become an independent state.

52. **E.** Lao Zi (604-531? BCE) was a contemporary of Confucius.

53. **D.** Skin color is the fundamental basis by which people in many societies sort out where they reside, attend school, and perform many daily activities.

54. **B.** Ethnicity is identity with a group of people that share distinct physical and mental traits as a product of common heredity and cultural traditions.

55. **C.** Hispanic Americans are clustered in the southwestern part of the United States.

56. **C.** Nationality is identity with a group of people who share legal attachment and personal allegiance to a particular place as a result of being born there.

57. **D.** A country like Chile or Italy has many areas isolated from the capital because they are elongated states.

58. **D.** See Figure 8-30 on page 278. Geometric boundaries are simply straight lines drawn on a map. The boundary between Chad and Libya was drawn by European countries early in the twentieth century, when the area comprised a series of colonies. This boundary is now disputed.

59. **A.** The Roman Empire controlled most of Europe, North Africa, and Southwestern Asia for nearly 1,000 years in the ancient world.

60. **E.** The purpose is to benefit the political party in power, although gerrymandering is now illegal.

61. **B.** This index looks at GDP, life expectancy, literacy rate, and educational level to determine a country's level of development.

62. See Figure 9-24 on page 313. The United Nations has found that in nearly every country, gender inequality has declined since the 1990s.

63. **E.** The main features that distinguish commercial agriculture from subsistence agriculture include the percentage of farmers in the labor force, the use of machinery, and farm size.

64. **C.** The Commonwealth includes the United Kingdom and 52 other states that were once British colonies.

65. **C.** Truck comes from the middle English word meaning bartering or the exchange of commodities. Truck farmers may sell their crops at a farmer's market, from the back of their trucks, or may sell to a large corporation.

66. **E.** *The Isolated State* explained that commercial farmers were most concerned with the cost of land versus the cost of transportation to markets, when deciding what and where to grow crops.

67. **E.** Scientists agree that agriculture originated in multiple hearths around the world.

68. **A.** Post-Fordist focuses on teams, problem solving, and leveling (equality among management and workers).

69. **D.** There are currently 362 metropolitan statistical areas in the United States.

70. **E.** This zone includes the suburbs, where high quality housing and good schools are located.

71. **D.** Gentrification has been an important process in many U.S. inner-city areas in recent years.

72. **A.** This is sometimes called a beltway.

73. **D.** Because of housing shortages, a large percentage of poor immigrants to urban areas in developing countries live in squatter settlements.

74. **E.** Fred Kniffen is an American cultural geographer.

75. **C.** Structural adjustment programs create conditions in less developed countries to encourage international trade. They involve raising taxes, reducing government spending, controlling inflation, and encouraging a more productive private sector.

Free Response:

1. **A.** In terms of development, Stage 1 countries are still in hunting and gathering societies, if they have any type of economy it would most likely be barter. Stage 2 are less developed countries that are starting to urbanize. Development would come from outside sources and be a source of jobs for citizens there. Stage 3 countries have experienced industrialization and see an emergence of a middle class that now is moving out of the overcrowded cities to suburbs. Stage 4 countries are advanced MDCs whose patterns of urbanization continue to be urban to suburban and who provided tertiary services the most.

B. Stage 2 country would be Cambodia because it has high NIR and is providing "sweat shops" for the world. Workers leave their farms to go work in the factories.
Stage 3 country would be Brazil, where workers are becoming specialized and are moving into cities to work in factories. Stage 4 country would be the United States, where workers still come in search of the American Dream

2. **A.** Call centers are also known as a call-answering job. Their main purpose is to answer questions posed by customers from all over the world. People may call to find their missing luggage or fix a problem on their computer.

B. Most call centers are located in places like India where the labor is cheap, many people speak English, and there are many people in need of jobs. These centers give people an opportunity to increase their income and thus help their family's livelihood.

3. A. In North Africa, Arabic acts as a centripetal force because it unites the people. It does not matter what nationality, ethnic group, or tribe they are from, they can at least communicate in the same language.

B. In a country like South Sudan, language becomes a centrifugal force because some people speak Arabic, Niger-Congo, or Niger-Saharan languages. The government might struggle to be able to communicate with its own people. Misunderstandings can occur because groups don't understand one another, and often the language of the people is tied to age-old ethnic conflicts.

Chapter Quick Quiz and Free Response Answers

Chapter 1:
1.1.1. B
1.1.2. C
1.2.1. C
1.2.2. C
1.3.1. C
1.3.2. C
1.4.1. D
1.4.2. C

Quick Quiz Answers:
1.1. E.
1.2. C.
1.3. C.
1.4. A.
1.5. E.
1.6. C.

Free Response Chapter 1:
A. The four types of distortion that can occur when you are creating a map deal with shape, distance, relative size, and direction.

B. Because geographers must take into account the fact that distortion will occur, they have created maps that adjust for each:
    1. Shape—the best map projection to deal with exaggerated shapes of countries would be a Mercator projection.
    2. Distance is also best on a Mercator projection especially near the equator.
    3. Relative size is best projected on equal-area projections.
    4. Direction is consistent on Mercator projections.

Chapter 2:
2.1.1. C
2.1.2. A
2.2.1. C
2.2.2. C
2.3.1. B
2.3.2. A
2.4.1. E
2.4.2. B

Quick Quiz Answers:
2.1. B.
2.2. C.
2.3. D.
2.4. E.
2.5. A.
2.6. B.
2.7. D.
2.8. D.

Free Response Chapter 2:
A. China, India, the Middle East, and parts of North Africa have more men than women according to the Sex Ratio Map.

B. This can be explained because in most of these countries, especially China, the culture value boys more than girls. Boys are thought to be the ones who will take care of their parents. In India girls are a burden for a family, as they have to come up with a dowry when she gets married. Muslim countries tend to look to sons to carry on the family name and business, so a girl is a burden.

C. Governments can make laws to protect young girls. They can encourage them to get an education and make it a crime if they are discriminated against. They can also give women political power so that they have a voice in the government and their lives.

Chapter 3 Answers:
3.1.1. E.
3.1.2. C.
3.2.1. D.
3.2.1. C.
3.3.1. E.
3.3.2. B.
3.4.1. D.
3.4.2. A.

Quick Quiz Answers:
3.1. E.
3.2. F.
3.3. B.
3.4. C.
3.5. G.
3.6. H.
3.7. D.
3.8. A.

Free Response Chapter 3:
A. China and the United States are both experiencing interregional migration.

B. One common characteristic for migration in both of these countries is job opportunities. People are forced to move in search of higher paying jobs and in some cases just to get a job.

C. In China, for instance, people are leaving the rural areas and flocking to the cities, so they are experiencing urbanization at a very rapid rate. In the United States people are leaving some cities, especially in the Northeast region, where people are leaving and moving to jobs in the south.

Chapter 4 Answers:
4.1.1. D.
4.1.2. E.
4.2.1. B.
4.2.2. D.
4.3.1. E.
4.3.2. E.

4.4.1. A.
4.4.2. B.

Quick Quiz Answers:
4.1 E.
4.2. A.
4.3 B.
4.4 Social media has more of an impact on both folk and popular culture today because of the easy access to it. If you watch the news during the Arab Spring, even Bedouins had smart phones and access to the situations/uprising during the government overthrows. These folk cultures were no longer kept in the dark about things that were going on in their country, they could actually watch them unfold in "real time."

Free Response Chapter 4:
A. By looking at the map, it is clear that soccer is truly taking off. What once was sport that was mainly found in England, as a folk culture in small villages, is now turning into a global phenomenon. The map illustrates how many years a country has qualified for the world cup.

B. While Europe and South America clearly have qualified for the World Cup for the most years, there are countries such as the United States, Australia, China, and Russia who are gaining ground. Even countries in Africa are catching up. What becomes clearer when looking at the map are the host countries; this is when we see the "snowballing" effect, where host nations are located all over the globe.

Chapter 5 Answers:
5.1.1. C.
5.1.2. C.
5.2.1. E.
5.2.2. C.
5.3.1. C.
5.3.2. D.
5.4.1. A.
5.4.2. D.

Quick Quiz Answers:
5.1. C.
5.2. A.
5.3 C.
5.4 D.
5.5. C.

Free Response Chapter 5:
There are many reasons why a government might have bilingual signs through out their country. (Here are some possible reasons.)
1. Cultural diversity—the government realizes that they should not be totally taken over by globalization and passes laws that will maintain their unique culture.

2. As is the case in Wales, the government passed laws to revitalize their language because it had the potential to become extinct.

3. Tourism is always enhanced when there is something unique about a country, making them a place people want to come and visit.

Chapter 6 answers:
6.1.1. D.
6.1.2. A.
6.2.1. C.
6.2.2. D.
6.3.1. D.
6.3.2. C.
6.4.1. D.
6.4.2. D.

Quick Quiz Answers:
6.1. A.
6.2. D.
6.3. E.
6.4. C.
6.5. B.

Free Response Chapter 6:
A. The photo shows a Buddha, which had been carved into the stone in Afghanistan many years ago. After the Taliban came to power, they tried to rid the cultural landscape of the country, as shown in the bottom photo where the Buddha has disappeared, as the Taliban tried to rid Afghanistan of any religion other than Islam.

B. Three reasons why religion causes problems are:
1. Religion conflicts with the government type that is in power, an example would be in the Soviet Union. Communist ideology does not embrace religion.
2. Religious conflicts can occur when it conflicts with the values of the people, as with the Taliban who denounced Western values.
3. Religions can cause conflict when it goes against customs of the majority of the people, for instance in India some people value the caste system, but Buddhists
renounce it.

Chapter 7 Answers:
7.1.1. A.
7.1.2. A.
7.2.1. D.
7.2.2. C.
7.3.1. D.
7.3.2. B.
7.4.1. C.
7.4.2. D.

Quick Quiz Answers:
7.1. B.
7.2. C.
7.3. A.
7.4. A.
7.5. C.
7.6. B.

Free Response Chapter 7:

A.   By looking at the map it is clear that ethnicities were forced to move after World War II.   For instance, Poles had to move to occupy areas of the Soviet Union and Germans were forced to move into areas of Poland.

B.   The migration does in fact impact nationalistic tendencies because Germans will always be loyal to Germany, even if they are living with in the boundaries of Poland.   They will never show true loyalty to the place they were forced to live and might even try to rebel against the government there.

C.   Ideally nation-states are countries that hold a homogeneous culture, like Korea.   When many ethnicities are made to live within one area, ethnic conflicts can occur, like the ethnic cleansing in former Yugoslavia.

Chapter 8 Answers:
8.1.1. D.
8.1.2. C.
8.2.1. D.
8.2.2. C.
8.3.1. B.
8.3.2. D.
8.4.1. E.
8.4.2. C.

Quick Quiz Answers
8.1 Korea
8.2. Antarctica
8.3. nation-state
8.4 Lithuania
8.5. geometric, ethnic
8.6. elongated
8.7. gerrymandering

Free Response Chapter 8:

1.   The UN grew in 1955 when countries that had been part of Nazi Germany gained independence.   It grew again in the 1960s when colonies, especially of France and Britain, gained independence.   Last, it grew around 1993 when the Cold War ended and former Soviet states gained independence.

2.   One positive outcome of these increases, is that democracy is spread and people gain freedom. Ultimately the world will see less human rights violations, hopefully.

Chapter 9 Answers:
9.1.1. D.
9.1.2. A.
9.2.1. C.
9.2.2. A.
9.3.1. D.
9.3.2. B.
9.4.1. D.
9.4.2. E.

Quick Quiz Answers:
9.1. C.
9.2. D.
9.3. B.
9.4. B.
9.5. D.

Free Response Chapter 9:
A. Countries with the highest income include: The United States, Canada, Saudi Arabia, Australia, the Scandinavian countries, countries in Western Europe. Countries which have a low Gender Inequality Index would also include the United States, Canada, Western Europe, Australia, the Scandinavian countries, but also China, and Tunisia would be included.

B. At first glance it seems that countries with high income also have low gender inequality.

C. A major exception to this rule would be found in China.

Chapter 10 Answers:
10.1.1. B.
10.1.2. E.
10.2.1. C.
10.2.2. C.
10.3.1. B.
10.3.2. E.
10.4.1. D.
10.4.2. A.

Quick Quiz Answers:
10.1. B.
10.2. C.
10.3. D.
10.4. E.
10.5. A.
10.6. C.

Free Response Chapter 10:
A. Commercial farmers in developed countries face many economic issues because farmers have become TOO successful in mass production. They can produce more food than is demanded.

B.   Governments can use strategies to help farmers.   These include encouraging farmers to avoid producing crops that are in great supply and to plant other crops to help replenish the soil. They also set target prices to help the farmers, where they pay the difference for the crops. Last they might actually purchase the surplus and donate it to poorer countries.

Chapter 11 Answers:
11.1.1. B.
11.1.2. A.
11.2.1. E.
11.2.2. E.
11.3.1. C.
11.3.2. D.

11.4.1. C.
11.4.2. A.

Quick Quiz Answers:
11.1. B.
11.2 A.
11.3. C.
11.4. B.
11.5. C.

Free Response Chapter 11:
A.   Containerization is the process of loading large cargo containers full of products that can be transferred to a number of different modes of transportation. Break of bulk point is the point where different modes of transportation might meet, like a harbor where a ship and a truck can meet and exchange the containers.

B.   The reason why companies would choose to take advantage of containerization and break of bulk points is simply to reduce costs of transportation while moving products efficiently.

Chapter 12 Answers:
12.1.1. B.
12.1.2. D.
12.2.1. D.
12.2.2. E.
12.3.1. E.
12.3.2. C.
12.4.1. B.
12.4.2. C.

Quick Quiz Answers:
12.1. Ur
12.2. Knossos
12.3. FIRE
12.4. hexagon
12.5. developing, developed

Free Response Chapter 12:
When looking at market area analysis, two terms, threshold and range, are very important geographic ideas. The range is how far people are willing to travel to obtain service, where the threshold is how many people (the minimum) need to use the service in order for it to be profitable.

One reason some services have larger ranges than others is because they provide specialized services, like cancer treatment. People are willing to travel much greater distances to obtain these services than they are to buy a pizza.

Chapter 13 Answers:
13.1.1. C.
13.1.2. E.
13.2.1. C.
13.2.2. A.
13.3.1. E.

13.3.2. B.
13.4.1. E.
13.4.2. A.

Quick Quiz Answers:
13.1. B.
13.2. A.
13.3. E.
13.4. C.
13.5. E.

Free Response Chapter 13:
A. Gentrification is the process of converting low-income rental properties near the CBD to middle class owner occupied homes.

B. Gentrification is a better solution for housing than urban sprawl because it is upgrading space that is already in use, rather than clearing arable land to build suburbs.

C. Middle class families would enjoy living nearer to their jobs, which historically would be in the CBD. Also this is where most cultural events occur, so they would be located close to museums and theaters, which also make the location attractive.